UNIVERSITY ASSOCIATES
Publishers and Consultants

SERIES IN HUMAN RELATIONS TRAINING

A Handbook of Structured Experiences for Human Relations Training

Volume I
(Revised)

Edited by

J. WILLIAM PFEIFFER, Ph.D.
Human Relations Consultant
La Jolla, California

JOHN E. JONES, Ph.D.
Human Relations Consultant
La Jolla, California

UNIVERSITY ASSOCIATES
Publishers and Consultants
7596 Eads Avenue
La Jolla, California 92037

Copyright © 1974 by International Authors, B.V.

First edition Copyright © 1969 by University Associates, Inc.

ISBN: 0-88390-041-6

Library of Congress Catalog Card Number 73-92840

Printed in the United States of America

PREFACE TO THE REVISED EDITION

In the five years since the first volume of *A Handbook of Structured Experiences for Human Relations Training* appeared, we have accumulated considerable experience with these materials. In addition to the four volumes of the *Handbook*, we have developed a companion publication—*The Annual Handbook for Group Facilitators*. This editorial activity has been accompanied by a wide array of experiences in consulting and in laboratories and workshops where we have experimented with many variations. We have also received numerous contributions from group facilitators. Some of these have been incorporated into revisions of the *Handbook*.

The *Handbook* has been revised in content and re-designed to have a more durable cover. Type faces have been selected which will allow clear photo-reproduction, both at the same size and in enlargements.

The structured experiences that appear in this book are the "folk music" of human relations. They fall into three major categories: (1) unadapted "classic" experiences, (2) highly adapted experiences, and (3) innovated experiences. Like folk music, the origins of most of these structured experiences are difficult to trace. They have been passed from facilitator to facilitator by word-of-mouth, on scraps of paper, and on unsigned, undated mimeographed sheets.

We have made considerable effort to determine the authorship of these materials, but we continue to have concern about the accuracy of our research into finding the people who developed particular exercises. An interesting phenomenon occurs in the human relations training field that aggravates the authorship problem. A facilitator uses a structured experience or an instrument for several years, it becomes a part of his training repertoire, and he forgets where he originally obtained it. When he sees another facilitator using a version of it, he feels that he is not being acknowledged for something which he "owns." As one consultant put it, "I have been using my own version for such a long time that I simply assumed it was the only one in the world."

Although the *Handbook* is copyrighted, there are few restrictions concerning the reproduction of its contents. Users should feel free to duplicate and/or modify the forms, charts, structured exercises, descriptions, and instruments for use in education/training designs. However, *reproduction of items from the book in publications for sale or large-scale distribution should be done only with the prior permission of the editors.* The intent is to make these materials widely available and useful. Occasionally someone asks whether we are concerned about this policy. Our response is that we wish more publishers would follow suit. It is widely known that copyrighted materials are duplicated for use in learning designs. We believe it is unnecessary to cause those who duplicate such materials to feel guilty.

This handbook is written by practitioners for practitioners. In the *Handbooks* and the *Annuals* we record the development of structured experiences, instruments, theoretical positions, and ideas for applications as they emerge. To that end we invite inquiries from facilitators about our policies regarding incorporating their work in future publications. Users are encouraged to submit structured experiences, instruments they have developed, and papers they have written which might be of interest to practitioners in human relations training. In this manner, our Series in Human Relations Training serves a clearinghouse function for ideas developed by group facilitators.

J. William Pfeiffer
John E. Jones

La Jolla, California
October, 1973

ABOUT UNIVERSITY ASSOCIATES
PUBLISHERS AND CONSULTANTS

UNIVERSITY ASSOCIATES is an educational organization engaged in human relations training, research, consulting, publication, and both pre-service and in-service education. The organization consists of educational consultants and experienced facilitators in human relations, leadership training, and organization development.

In addition to offering general laboratory experiences, University Associates designs and carries out programs on a contractual basis for various organizations. These programs fall under the following areas of specialization: Human Relations Training, Leadership Development, Organization Development, Community Development, and Educational Research.

Structured experiences in University Associates publications are numbered consecutively. Structured experiences 1 through 24 are in *Volume I*, numbers 25 through 48 are in *Volume II*, numbers 49 through 74 in *Volume III*, 75 through 87 in *The 1972 Annual Handbook for Group Facilitators*, 88 through 100 in the *1973 Annual*, and 101 through 124 in *Volume IV*. These numbers are used for the same exercise when books are revised, even though the title of the exercise or some details may be changed.

TABLE OF CONTENTS

Page

INTRODUCTION TO THE REVISED EDITION

Since its inception, University Associates has become involved with or had experience in nearly every facet of human relations training. With these experiences, we have grown personally and have found our philosophies to be evolving continuously as our awareness of the impact and methodology of human relations grows.

Spontaneous experiences within a group training setting may be valuable in terms of awareness expansion and emotional freedom. However, they may not produce as much personal growth and solid, transferable learning as does a structured experience, designed to focus on individual behavior, constructive feedback, processing, and psychological integration.

Our interest in providing a distinctive model of human relations training has resulted in an increasing orientation within our consulting activities, laboratories, and workshops toward experiences which will produce generally predictable outcomes. In designing experiences, we strive to examine specific needs of a client system or group and then develop learning situations to meet these needs. We believe that this concern for learning needs should be the minimum expectation of any individual participating in a training event. Therefore, all of our training designs incorporate structure to facilitate learning.

Our use of and experimentation with structured experiences have led to an interest in developing useful, uncomplicated questionnaires and other instruments. Each volume of the *Handbook* contains structured experiences that include instruments. Many commercially available instruments are being used more and more in our laboratory designs. We published *Instrumentation in Human Relations Training* by Pfeiffer and Heslin in June, 1973, to share information about the use of these materials. We find that the complementary use of structured experiences and instruments can create powerful learning environments. We encourage those in human relations training to become acquainted with this two-fold approach.

The adaptability of both structured experiences and instruments in creating highly functional training designs has emerged as a chief consideration in publishing materials. One norm in human relations training activities is innovation. Therefore, the structured experiences in these handbooks can easily be adapted to fit a particular training design. As one friend remarked of the handbook, "I use it all of the time, but I almost never do things the way you guys describe them."

Our awareness of the infinite variety of experiences which can be produced in adapting these materials becomes more specifically focused the longer we work in human relations. Therefore, in revising the *Handbook*, we have added a section entitled "Variations" to the structured experiences format. Hopefully, the variations we suggest will trigger other adaptation ideas.

In addition, we cross-reference experiences which supplement or complement each other. We also incorporate references to appropriate lecturettes and other materials from our *Annual Handbook for Group Facilitators*. The facilitator may use the "Notes" section in this book as a starting point for adaptation.

The purpose, then, of the *Handbook* is to share training materials we have found to be viable in training designs. Part of the experiences were originated within University Associates, and part were submitted by facilitators in the field. It is gratifying that facilitators around the world are using the *Handbook* and concur with the philosophy that sharing these valuable materials is more in the spirit of human relations theory than the stagnating concept of "ownership" of ideas.

As in other volumes of the *Handbook*, content is arranged, for the most part, in order of the increasing understanding, skill, and experience needed by the facilitator. The first structured experience, therefore, requires much less background of the facilitator than does the last. The earlier experiences generate less affect and less data than do those near the end of the book; consequently the facilitator needs less skill in processing to use them effectively and responsibly.

A concern we bring to all our training publications is the need for adequate processing of any human relations training experience, so that participants are able to integrate learning without stress generated by unresolved feelings and/or lack of understanding. At this point the expertise of the facilitator becomes crucial if the experience is to be responsive to the learning and emotional needs of the participants. The facilitator must decide whether he will be able to process successfully the data which emerges.

Any facilitator, regardless of his background, who is committed to the growth of individuals in his group can usefully employ these structured experiences. The choice of activities should be made by two criteria—the facilitator's competence and the participants' needs.

1. LISTENING AND INFERRING: A GETTING-ACQUAINTED ACTIVITY

Goal

To facilitate the involvement of individuals in a newly formed group.

Group Size

Unlimited number of triads.

Time Required

Fifteen minutes.

Physical Setting

Triads separate from one another, as far as possible, to avoid noise interference.

Process

I. Triads are formed. The criterion for formation is not knowing the other members of the triad.

II. Participants in each group name themselves A, B, or C.

1. Participant A takes three minutes to tell the other two persons as much about himself as he feels comfortable in doing. Then B and C take two minutes to tell A what they heard him say. They also tell him what they infer (or assume) from what he said or left unsaid.

2. The process is repeated, with participant B telling about himself. A and C then tell what they heard and inferred.

3. In the final round participant C tells about himself, and A and B repeat what they heard and tell their inferences.

Variations

I. All three participants can tell about themselves before the others respond.

II. After each participant tells about himself, the communication becomes two-way in order for the listeners to check on the accuracy of their listening and inferring.

III. The two listeners can be assigned different tasks. One listens to make a paraphrase, and the other listens to draw inferences.

IV. The content can be changed from getting acquainted to exploring points of view about an issue that is relevant to the group.

Similar Structured Experiences: *Vol. I:* Structured Experience **5, 8;** *Vol. III:* **49, 65;** *'72 Annual:* **75;** *'73 Annual:* **87, 88;** *Vol. IV:* **101, 120.**

Notes on the use of "Listening and Inferring":

2. TWO-FOUR-EIGHT: BUILDING TEAMS

Goal

To divide a large group into workable subgroups in such a way as to increase group cohesiveness and identity.

Group Size

Any number. The example is based on thirty-two participants who are divided into four groups. This design is easily adaptable to groups of other sizes.

Time Required

Approximately thirty minutes.

Physical Setting

Participants should sit on chairs which can be moved easily as groups form.

Process

I. Participants are asked to number themselves off using 'one, two, one, two," etc., in order to form two large groups.

II. Participants labeled "one" are asked to stand on one side of the room and those labeled "two" on the other side.

III. Each number one invites a number two to form a dyad. Number ones are asked to invite someone they do not know or, if they know all participants, someone they do not know well. Dyads move to a neutral location until all have been formed.

IV. The facilitator divides the dyads into two groups of eight dyads each, which relocate on opposite sides of the room.

V. After a consultation which should take no more than three minutes, a dyad from one side of the room invites a dyad from the opposite side of the room to form a quartet. A dyad may not decline an invitation to join another dyad. One by one, dyads from the same side of the room issue invitations until all eight quartets are formed.

VI. The quartets then caucus for no more than three minutes to determine which other quartet they would like to join.

VII. Quartets successively ask another quartet to join them. Invitations to join *may* be declined. If an invitation is declined, the next group makes its offer. This process continues until all quartets have been chosen.

VIII. The octets are now ready to work. Their first task is to discuss the experience of choosing and being chosen.

Variations

I. Invitations to join may be rejected in forming the various groupings.

II. To achieve maximum heterogeneity, participants are urged to invite only the persons they know least well. After octets are formed, the facilitator shifts membership to get an even representation in each group based on some relevant criteria, such as no supervisor and subordinate in the same group, proportional representation by males and females, or age. The criteria can be announced prior to the invitations or following.

III. Open-ended statements can be provided at each stage of the teams' formation to heighten the developmental process. Examples:

> Dyads—I chose you because . . .
> > When you chose me, I felt . . .
> Quartets—We chose you because . . .
> > Our reaction to being chosen was . . .
> Octets—My first impression of you was . . .
> > Right now I'm feeling . . .

Similar Structured Experiences: *Vol. II:* Structured Experience **27**; *Vol. III:* **66**; *Vol. IV:* **118**.
Lecturette Source: *'73 Annual:* "A Model of Group Development."

Notes on the use of "Two-Four-Eight":

3. T-P LEADERSHIP QUESTIONNAIRE: AN ASSESSMENT OF STYLE

Goal

To evaluate oneself in terms of task orientation and people orientation.

Group Size

Unlimited.

Time Required

Approximately forty-five minutes.

Materials

I. T-P Leadership Questionnaire for each participant.

II. Pencil for each participant.

III. T-P Leadership-Style Profile Sheet for each participant.

Physical Setting

Participants should be seated at tables or desk chairs.

Process

I. Without prior discussion, the facilitator asks participants to fill out the T-P Leadership Questionnaire.

II. Before the questionnaires are scored, the facilitator presents a brief lecturette on shared leadership as a function of the combined concern for task and people.

III. The facilitator announces that, in order to locate himself on the Leadership-Style Profile Sheet, each group participant will score his own questionnaire on the dimensions of task orientation (T) and people orientation (P).

IV. The facilitator instructs the participants in the scoring as follows:

1. Circle the item number for items 8, 12, 17, 18, 19, 30, 34, and 35.

2. Write the number 1 in front of a *circled item number* if you responded S (seldom) or N (never) to that item.

3. Also write a number 1 in front of *item numbers not circled* if you responded A (always) or F (frequently).

4. Circle the number 1's which you have written in front of the following items: 3, 5, 8, 10, 15, 18, 19, 22, 24, 26, 28, 30, 32, 34, and 35.

5. *Count the circled number 1's.* This is your score for concern for people. Record the score in the blank following the letter P at the end of the questionnaire.

6. *Count the uncircled number 1's.* This is your score for concern for task. Record this number in the blank following the letter T.

V. The facilitator distributes the Leadership-Style Profile Sheet and instructs participants to follow the directions on the sheet. He then leads a discussion of implications members attach to their location on the profile.

Variations

I. Participants can predict how they will appear on the profile prior to scoring the questionnaire.

II. Paired participants already acquainted can predict each other's scores. If they are not acquainted, they can discuss their reactions to the questionnaire items to form some bases for this prediction.

III. The leadership styles represented on the profile sheet can be illustrated through role-playing. A relevant situation can be set up, and the "leaders" can be coached to demonstrate the styles being studied.

IV. Subgroups can be formed of participants similarly situated on the shared leadership scale. These groups can be assigned identical tasks to perform. The data generated can be processed in terms of morale and productivity.

Similar Structured Experiences: *Vol. I:* Structured Experience **12;** *Vol. II:* **38.**
Similar Instruments: *'72 Annual:* "Supervisory Attitudes: The X-Y Scale," "Intervention Style Survey"; *'73 Annual:* "LEAD."
Lecturette Sources: *'72 Annual:* "Notes on Freedom"; W.R. Lassey, *Leadership and Social Change* (University Associates, 1971).

Notes on the use of "T-P Leadership Questionnaire":

The T–P Leadership Questionnaire was adapted from Sergiovanni, Metzcus, and Burden's revision of the Leadership Behavior Description Questionnaire, *American Educational Research Journal* 6 (1969), pages 62-79.

Structured Experience 3

T–P LEADERSHIP QUESTIONNAIRE

Name_____ Group_____

Directions: The following items describe aspects of leadership behavior. Respond to each item according to the way you would most likely act if you were the leader of a work group. Circle whether you would most likely behave in the described way: always (A), frequently (F), occasionally (O), seldom (S), or never (N).

A F O S N 1. I would most likely act as the spokesman of the group.

A F O S N 2. I would encourage overtime work.

A F O S N 3. I would allow members complete freedom in their work.

A F O S N 4. I would encourage the use of uniform procedures.

A F O S N 5. I would permit the members to use their own judgment in solving problems.

A F O S N 6. I would stress being ahead of competing groups.

A F O S N 7. I would speak as a representative of the group.

A F O S N 8. I would needle members for greater effort.

A F O S N 9. I would try out my ideas in the group.

A F O S N 10. I would let the members do their work the way they think best.

A F O S N 11. I would be working hard for a promotion.

A F O S N 12. I would tolerate postponement and uncertainty.

A F O S N 13. I would speak for the group if there were visitors present.

A F O S N 14. I would keep the work moving at a rapid pace.

A F O S N 15. I would turn the members loose on a job and let them go to it.

A F O S N 16. I would settle conflicts when they occur in the group.

A F O S N 17. I would get swamped by details.

A F O S N 18. I would represent the group at outside meetings.

A F O S N 19. I would be reluctant to allow the members any freedom of action.

A F O S N 20. I would decide what should be done and how it should be done.

A   F   O   S   N   21. I would push for increased production.

A   F   O   S   N   22. I would let some members have authority which I could keep.

A   F   O   S   N   23. Things would usually turn out as I had predicted.

A   F   O   S   N   24. I would allow the group a high degree of initiative.

A   F   O   S   N   25. I would assign group members to particular tasks.

A   F   O   S   N   26. I would be willing to make changes.

A   F   O   S   N   27. I would ask the members to work harder.

A   F   O   S   N   28. I would trust the group members to exercise good judgment.

A   F   O   S   N   29. I would schedule the work to be done.

A   F   O   S   N   30. I would refuse to explain my actions.

A   F   O   S   N   31. I would persuade others that my ideas are to their advantage.

A   F   O   S   N   32. I would permit the group to set its own pace.

A   F   O   S   N   33. I would urge the group to beat its previous record.

A   F   O   S   N   34. I would act without consulting the group.

A   F   O   S   N   35. I would ask that group members follow standard rules and regulations.

T _____   P _____

Structured Experience 3

T-P LEADERSHIP-STYLE PROFILE SHEET

Name_____   Group_____

Directions: To determine your style of leadership, mark your score on the *concern for task* dimension (T) on the left-hand arrow below. Next, move to the right-hand arrow and mark your score on the *concern for people* dimension (P). Draw a straight line that intersects the P and T scores. The point at which that line crosses the *shared leadership* arrow indicates your score on that dimension.

**SHARED LEADERSHIP RESULTS FROM
BALANCING CONCERN FOR TASK AND CONCERN FOR PEOPLE**

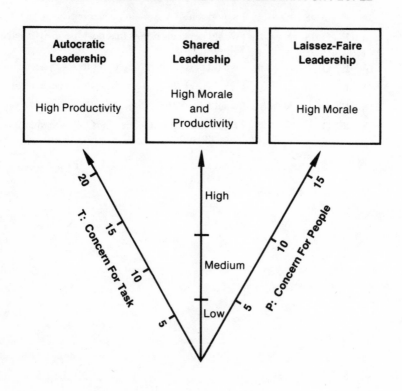

4. ONE-WAY, TWO-WAY:
A COMMUNICATIONS EXPERIMENT

Goals

I. To conceptualize the superior functioning of two-way communication through participatory demonstration.

II. To examine the application of communication in family, social, and occupational settings.

Group Size

Unlimited.

Time Required

Approximately forty-five minutes.

Materials

I. Newsprint and felt-tipped marker.

II. Two sheets of paper and a pencil for each participant.

III. A reproduction of Diagram I and Diagram II for the demonstrator.

Physical Setting

Participants should be seated facing the demonstrator, but in such a way that it will be difficult, if not impossible, to see each other's drawings.

Process

I. The facilitator may wish to begin with a discussion about ways of looking at communication in terms of content, direction, networks, or interference.

II. The facilitator explains that the group will experiment with the directional aspects of communication by participating in the following exercise:

1. The facilitator selects a demonstrator and one or two observers. The remaining participants each are supplied with a pencil and two sheets of

paper. They are instructed to label one sheet Diagram I and the other Diagram II.

2. The facilitator tells the group that the demonstrator will give them directions for drawing a series of squares. Participants are instructed to draw the squares exactly as the demonstrator tells them, on the paper labeled Diagram I. Participants may neither ask questions nor give audible responses.

3. The demonstrator is asked to study the arrangement of squares in Diagram I for two minutes.

4. The facilitator instructs the observers to take notes on the behavior and reactions of the demonstrator and/or the participants.

5. The facilitator prepares the following three tables on newsprint.

TABLE 1
(For Diagram I)

Number Correct	Estimate	Actual
5		
4		
3		
2		
1		
0		

TABLE 2
(For Diagram II)

Number Correct	Estimate	Actual
5		
4		
3		
2		
1		
0		

TABLE 3
(Summary)

	Diagram I	Diagram II
Time Elapsed		
Estimated Median		
Actual Median		

6. The facilitator asks the demonstrator to turn his back to the group or to stand behind a screen. The facilitator then asks him to proceed, reminding him to tell the group what to draw as quickly and as accurately as he can. The facilitator again cautions the group not to ask questions.

7. The time it takes the demonstrator to complete his instructions is recorded in the summary Table 3 under Diagram I.

8. Each participant is asked to estimate the number of squares he has drawn correctly in relation to the other squares. The facilitator then tabulates the participants' estimates in Table I.

9. The first phase of the experience is repeated with the following modifications: The demonstrator uses Diagram II, he faces the group, and he is allowed to respond to questions from the group. The participants should use the papers labeled Diagram II.

10. The facilitator has each of the participants estimate the number of squares he has drawn correctly in the second phase of the exercise and tabulates the estimates on Table 2. The facilitator then uses Tables 1 and 2 to calculate the median (or average) estimated accuracy for both Diagram I and Diagram II. He posts these medians in Table 3.

11. The group is then shown the actual diagrams for the two sets of squares. Each participant counts the number of squares he has drawn correctly on each diagram.

12. In the last columns of Tables 1 and 2, the facilitator tabulates the number of squares the participants have drawn correctly for each diagram. From the data, he determines the medians for Diagrams I and II and enters these in Table 3.

III. The facilitator leads a discussion of the results in terms of time, accuracy, and level of confidence, calling upon "back-home" experience and application.

IV. The observers report their process observations. The group discusses these in relation to the data generated during the first phase of the discussion.

Variations

I. Instead of medians, means (arithmetic averages) may be computed.

II. Additional phases such as the following can be included:

1. Two-way, with demonstrator facing participants, who are permitted to react nonverbally.

2. Two-way, with demonstrator not facing participants.

Structured Experience 4

III. Two or more participants can be selected to work together as a demonstration team.

IV. Teams of participants can be formed to draw the diagrams on newsprint cooperatively.

V. The content can be changed to include data relevant to the objectives of the training and/or a more complex type of problem.

VI. Physical models, made of dominoes or blocks, can be described by the demonstrator.

Lecturette Sources: *'72 Annual:* "Communication Modes: An Experiential Lecture"; *'73 Annual:* "Conditions Which Hinder Effective Communication."

Notes on the use of "One-Way, Two-Way":

The structured experience is adapted from H.J. Leavitt's *Managerial Psychology* (Chicago: University of Chicago Press, 1958), pages 118-28.

DIAGRAM I: ONE-WAY COMMUNICATION

Instructions: Study the series of squares below. With your back to the group, you are to direct the participants in how they are to draw the figures. Begin with the top square and describe each in succession, taking particular note of the relationship of each to the preceding one. No questions are allowed.

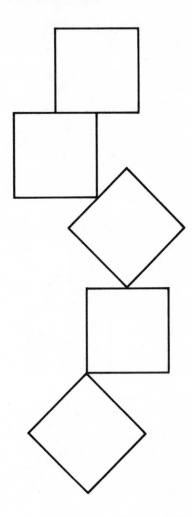

Structured Experience 4

DIAGRAM II: TWO-WAY COMMUNICATION

Instructions: Study the series of squares below. Facing the group, you are to direct the participants in how they are to draw the figures. Begin with the top square and describe each in succession, taking particular note of the relation of each to the preceding one. Answer all questions from participants and repeat if necessary.

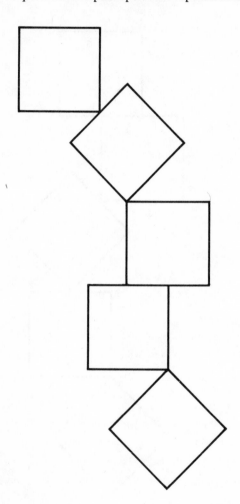

5. WHO AM I?: A GETTING-ACQUAINTED ACTIVITY

Goal

To allow participants to become acquainted quickly in a relatively non-threatening way.

Group Size

Unlimited.

Time Required

Approximately forty-five minutes.

Materials

I. For each participant: one 8½" x 11" sheet of paper with the question "Who am I?" written in one-inch letters at the top.

II. Pencil for each participant.

III. Piece of masking tape, a safety pin, or a straight pin for each participant.

Physical Setting

Large room in which participants may move freely.

Process

I. Participants receive the materials and are allowed ten minutes in which to write ten different answers to the question, "Who am I?" The facilitator should stress legibility, because participants must be able to read these answers easily from a distance.

II. Each participant fastens his completed sheet to the front of his clothing.

III. Participants circulate in a cocktail-party fashion, but *without* speaking. They are instructed to make eye contact with each person they encounter.

IV. The facilitator asks participants to move on to another person about every two minutes.

V. After this nonverbal phase, participants are told to return to two or three different people they thought would be interesting. They may now talk with each
other. They may be encouraged to ask questions which they ordinarily would not.

Variations

I. Instead of the question "Who am I?," participants can be instructed to complete
the open-ended statement, "I am becoming the kind of person who. . . ." Another
focus can be made by using the incomplete sentence, "I am pretending that. . . ."
(It is important that at least ten different responses be called for, so that participants move beyond superficial self-disclosure.)

II. Participants may be asked to avoid giving demographic data in their answers.
The facilitator may illustrate by pointing out the difference between "What am
I?" (husband, father, counselor, etc.) and "Who am I?" (tense, a taker of risks,
managing myself toward openness, etc.).

III. Self-descriptive adjectives can be called for instead of answers to the question. A
second column of adjectives could be in response to the question, "How would I
like to be?"

IV. Participants may be permitted to speak in Process step III.

V. After the processing, participants can tape their sheets to a wall, so that the complete getting-acquainted data are available for study at all times. Persons may be
encouraged to edit their sheets at any time during the training event.

VI. As a closure activity, participants may be instructed to write what they learned
during the training. The type of learning or topic may vary. For example, in a
personal growth laboratory the topic can be, "What I learned about me"; in a
leadership/management development laboratory, the topic could simply be,
"What I learned" or "What I am going to do differently."

Similar Structured Experiences: *Vol. I:* Structured Experience **1, 13, 20;** *Vol. II:* **42, 47;** *Vol. III:* **49;**
'73 Annual: **87, 88, 90, 99;** *Vol. IV:* **101, 109.**
Lecturette Sources: *'73 Annual:* "Johari Window," "Risk-Taking."

Notes on the use of "Who Am I?":

6. GROUP-ON-GROUP:*
A FEEDBACK EXPERIENCE

Goals

    I. To develop skills in process observation.

    II. To develop skills in giving appropriate feedback to individual group members.

Group Size

    Two groups of five to twelve participants each. More than one pair of groups may be directed simultaneously.

Time Required

    Approximately one hour.

Physical Setting

    The two groups sit in concentric circles facing inward, as shown in the following diagram. Participant "A" is observed by "a," "B" by "b," etc.

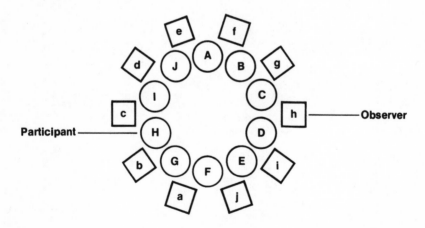

---

    *This structured experience is commonly referred to as a "fishbowl" design. The term "group-on-group" has less threatening connotations.

Process

I. The facilitator instructs participants to seat themselves according to the diagram. Then he explains the goals of the exercise and the general sequence of activities.

II. The facilitator instructs members of the outer circle to observe individuals' effects on group process and on group task accomplishment.

III. The inner-circle group participates in an activity chosen by the facilitator.

IV. After about ten minutes, the facilitator asks the participants in the inner circle to caucus with their observers. The facilitator instructs observers to give feedback in accordance with the criteria of effective feedback, as described in "Openness, Collusion, and Feedback," *The 1972 Annual Handbook for Group Facilitators*, page 199.

V. The process is then reversed so that observers now become inner-circle participants. New dyads should be formed to minimize retribution.

VI. The facilitator introduces another activity, and the process is repeated.

VII. The facilitator reassembles the entire group and leads a discussion of the process.

Variations

I. Observers may be briefed by a co-facilitator in a separate room.

II. Any of several behavior checklists may be used by observers. (For example, see *Vol. II*, Structured Experience 38.)

III. Two rounds of interaction can be experienced by each group. This permits observations about the effects of the feedback.

Similar Structured Experiences: *Vol. I:* Structured Experience **10;** *Vol. II:* **37;** *Vol. III:* **57;** *'72 Annual:* **79;** *'73 Annual:* **92.**
Lecturette Sources; *'72 Annual:* "Openness, Collusion, and Feedback"; *'73 Annual:* "Hill Interaction Matrix (HIM): Conceptual Framework for Understanding Groups."

Notes on the use of "Group-on-Group":

7. BROKEN SQUARES:
NONVERBAL PROBLEM-SOLVING

Goals

I. To analyze some aspects of cooperation in solving a group problem.

II. To sensitize participants to behaviors which may contribute toward or obstruct the solving of a group problem.

Group Size

Any number of groups of six participants each. There are five participants and an observer/judge in each group.

Time Required

Approximately forty-five minutes.

Materials

I. A set of broken squares (prepared according to directions following) for each group of five participants.

II. One copy for each group of the Broken Squares Group Instruction Sheet.

III. One copy for each observer of the Broken Squares Observer/Judge Instruction Sheet.

Physical Setting

A table that will seat five participants is needed for each group. Tables should be spaced far enough apart so that no group can see the puzzle-solving results of other groups.

Process

I. The facilitator begins with a discussion of the meaning of cooperation; this should lead to hypotheses about what is essential to successful group cooperation in problem-solving. The facilitator indicates that the group will conduct an experiment to test these hypotheses. Points such as the following are likely to emerge:

1. Each individual should understand the total problem.

2. Each individual should understand how he can contribute toward solving the problem.

3. Each individual should be aware of the potential contributions of other individuals.

4. There is a need to recognize the problems of other individuals in order to aid them in making their maximum contribution.

5. Groups that pay attention to their own problem-solving processes are likely to be more effective than groups that do not.

II. The facilitator forms groups of five participants plus the observer/judge. These observers are each given a copy of the Broken Squares Observer/Judge Instruction Sheet. The facilitator then asks each group to distribute among its members the set of broken squares (five envelopes). The envelopes are to remain unopened until the signal to begin work is given.

III. The facilitator gives to each group a copy of the Broken Squares Group Instruction Sheet. The facilitator reads these instructions to the group, calling for questions or questioning groups about their understanding of the instructions.

IV. He then tells the groups to begin work. It is important that the facilitator monitor tables during the exercise to enforce rules established in the instructions.

V. When all groups have completed the task, the facilitator engages the groups in a discussion of the experience. Observations are solicited from observers/judges. The facilitator encourages the groups to relate this experience to their "back-home" situations.

Variations:

I. When one member makes a square and fails to cooperate with the remaining members, the other four can be formed into two-person subgroups to make squares of the leftover pieces. They discuss their results, and the exercise is resumed.

II. The five-person teams can be given consultation assistance by the observer/judge or by one appointed member of the team. This may be a person who has done the exercise before.

III. Ten-person teams can be formed, with two duplicate sets of five squares each distributed among them. Teams of six to nine persons can be formed; in this case, prepare a broken square set with one square for each person, duplicating as many of the five squares as necessary.

IV. An intergroup competition can be established, with appropriate recognition to the group that solves the problem first.

V. Members may be permitted to talk during the problem-solving, or one member may be given permission to speak.

VI. Members may be permitted to write messages to each other during the problem-solving.

Similar Structured Experiences: *Vol. I:* Structured Experience **12;** *Vol. II:* **29, 31, 32, 33;** *Vol. III:* **54;** *'72 Annual:* **80;** *Vol. IV:* **102, 103, 105, 117.**

Notes on the use of "Broken Squares":

Adapted with permission from Alex Bavelas, Communication patterns in task-oriented groups, *Journal of the Acoustical Society of America,* 1950, *22,* 225-230. See also Bavelas, The five squares problem: An instructional aid in group cooperation, *Studies in Personnel Psychology,* 1973, *5,* 29-38. Variations I-IV were submitted by Tom Isgar, Case Western Reserve University, Cleveland, Ohio.

Structured Experience 7

DIRECTIONS FOR MAKING A SET OF BROKEN SQUARES

A set consists of five envelopes containing pieces of cardboard cut into different patterns which, when properly arranged, will form five squares of equal size. One set should be provided for each group of five persons.

To prepare a set, cut out five cardboard squares, each exactly 6″ × 6″. Place the squares in a row and mark them as below, penciling the letters lightly so they can be erased.

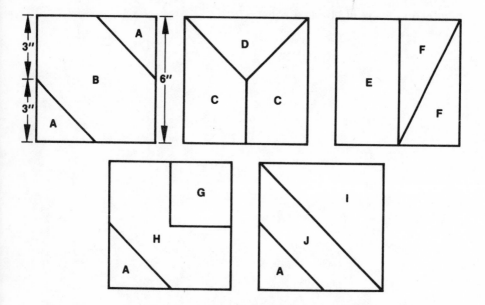

The lines should be so drawn that, when the pieces are cut out, those marked A will be exactly the same size, all pieces marked C the same size, etc. Several combinations are possible that will form one or two squares, but only one combination will form all five squares, each 6″×6″. After drawing the lines on the squares and labeling the sections with letters, cut each square along the lines into smaller pieces to make the parts of the puzzle.

Label the five envelopes 1, 2, 3, 4, and 5. Distribute the cardboard pieces into the five envelopes as follows: envelope 1 has pieces I, H, E; 2 has A, A, A, C; 3 has A, J; 4 has D, F; and 5 has G, B, F, C.

Erase the penciled letter from each piece and write, instead, the number of the envelope it is in. This makes it easy to return the pieces to the proper envelope, for subsequent use, after a group has completed the task.

Each set may be made from a different color of cardboard.

BROKEN SQUARES GROUP INSTRUCTION SHEET

Each of you has an envelope which contains pieces of cardboard for forming squares. When the facilitator gives the signal to begin, the task of your group is to form *five squares of equal size.* The task will not be completed until each individual has before him a perfect square of the same size as those in front of the other group members.

Specific limitations are imposed upon your group during this exercise.

1. No member may speak.

2. No member may ask another member for a piece or in any way signal that another person is to give him a piece. (Members may voluntarily give pieces to other members.)

BROKEN SQUARES OBSERVER/JUDGE INSTRUCTION SHEET

Your job is part observer and part judge. As a judge, you should make sure each participant observes the following rules:

1. There is to be no talking, pointing, or any other kind of communicating.

2. Participants may *give* pieces directly to other participants but may not *take* pieces from other members.

3. Participants may not place their pieces into the center for others to take.

4. It is permissible for a member to give away all the pieces to his puzzle, even if he has already formed a square.

As an observer, look for the following.

1. Who is willing to give away pieces of the puzzle?

2. Does anyone finish "his" puzzle and then withdraw from the group problem-solving?

3. Is there anyone who continually struggles with his pieces, yet is unwilling to give any or all of them away?

4. How many people are actively engaged in putting the pieces together?

5. What is the level of frustration and anxiety?

6. Is there any turning point at which the group begins to cooperate?

7. Does anyone try to violate the rules by talking or pointing as a means of helping fellow members solve the problem?

8. LISTENING TRIADS: BUILDING COMMUNICATIONS SKILLS

Goal

I. To develop skills in active listening.

II. To study barriers to effective listening.

Group Size

Unlimited number of triads.

Time Required

Approximately forty-five minutes.

Materials

I. Listening Triads Topics for Discussion Sheet for each participant.

II. Listening Triads Questions for Discussion Sheet for each participant.

Physical Setting

Room large enough for triads to be seated apart to avoid noise interference.

Process

I. The facilitator briefly discusses the goals of the activity.

II. Triads are formed.

III. Participants in each triad identify themselves as A, B, or C.

IV. The facilitator distributes copies of the Topics for Discussion Sheet.

V. The following instructions are given by the facilitator:

1. Participant A is the first speaker and chooses the topic to be discussed from those listed.

2. Participant B is the first listener.

3. Participant C is the first referee.

4. The topic chosen is to be discussed by the speaker. It is important that he be sensitive to the capacity of the listener. They can establish nonverbal cues for pacing the discussion.

5. The listener must summarize in his own words and without notes.

6. If the summary is thought to be incorrect, both the speaker and the referee are free to interrupt and correct any misunderstanding.

7. The referee is to make certain that the listener does not omit, distort, add to, respond to, or interpret what the speaker has said.

8. The total process of speaking and summarizing shall take seven minutes in each round.

VI. Round 1 is begun. The facilitator stops the process after seven minutes and responds to procedural questions.

VII. Participant B then becomes the speaker, participant C the listener, and participant A the referee. The new speaker chooses his Topic and begins. Round 2 should also take seven minutes.

VIII. Then C becomes the speaker, A the listener, and B the referee. After seven minutes, the discussion in Round 3 ends.

IX. The facilitator distributes copies of the Listening Triads Questions for Discussion Sheet, and triads discuss their process. Then generalizations about barriers to effective listening are elicited from the entire group.

Variations

I. Topics for discussion may be generated within the group. The facilitator may ask, "What are some topics about which there is likely to be disagreement within this group?" Suggestions are posted for use in the exercise.

II. Participant expectations about the training event can be discussed within the listening triads format.

III. Instead of only one speaker during each of the three rounds, there can be two speakers. Each must paraphrase what he hears before he responds. (The role of referee rotates from round to round.)

IV. Instead of telling the speaker what is heard, the listener can report what he remembers to the referee, with the speaker free to interrupt.

V. A fourth round can be added, in which each of the participants both speaks about and listens to another topic. This three-way conversation is a practice session for using what is learned in the earlier rounds.

VI. Whenever two participants do not seem to be speaking and/or listening effectively to each other, the facilitator may referee or ask the entire group to referee.

VII. During Round 1, the listener can be instructed to "parrot" the speaker, repeating word-for-word. In the second round the listener paraphrases, and in the third round the listener reflects the feelings being expressed by the speaker. A final round incorporates all three listening modes.

Similar Structured Experiences: *Vol. I:* Structured Experience **1, 4, 21;** *Vol. II:* **25;** *Vol. III:* **52, 66, 70;** *'73 Annual:* **87;** *Vol. IV:* **118.**
Lecturette Sources: *'72 Annual:* "Communication Modes: An Experiential Lecture"; *'73 Annual:* "Conditions Which Hinder Effective Communication," "Thinking and Feeling."

Notes on the use of "Listening Triads":

LISTENING TRIADS TOPICS FOR DISCUSSION SHEET

Each speaker chooses *one* topic.

1. Capital punishment
2. Prison reform
3. Drug use and abuse
4. Women's liberation
5. Foreign policy
6. Ecology
7. The new morality
8. Interracial marriage
9. Premarital and extramarital sex
10. Cohabitation
11. All-volunteer army
12. Political reform
13. Divorce
14. Homosexuality
15. The open classroom
16. The profit motive

LISTENING TRIADS QUESTIONS FOR DISCUSSION SHEET

1. What difficulties did you experience in each of the roles—speaker, listener, and referee?
2. What barriers to effective listening emerged during the exercise?
3. What did you learn about the effectiveness of your self-expression?
4. What applications might you make of this paraphrasing technique?

9. COMMITTEE MEETING: DEMONSTRATING HIDDEN AGENDAS

Goal

To illustrate the effects of hidden agendas on task accomplishment in a work group.

Group Size

Fifteen or more participants.

Time Required

Approximately one-and-a-half hours.

Materials

I. Copies of the Committee Meeting Problem Sheet and the Instructions for Playing a Role for all participants.

II. One Copy of the Committee Meeting Role Briefing Sheet, cut into strips to separate the role descriptions. Give one role to each committee member in some way that prevents members from knowing each other's "hidden agendas."

III. A copy of the Committee Meeting Role-Play Observation Sheet for each role-player observer.

IV. A copy of the Committee Meeting Process Observation Sheet for each group-process observer.

V. Pencils for all observers.

Physical Setting

The five role players are seated in the center, with all other participants seated around them. (A table in the center for the role players is optional.) Each of the five role-player observers sits directly across from the committee member whom he is observing. Group-process observers sit behind the role-player observers. The total setting takes the form of three concentric circles, as illustrated.

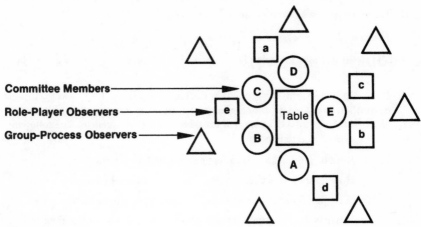

Committee Members
Role-Player Observers
Group-Process Observers

Process

I. The facilitator forms a committee of five people as role players and distributes to each of them a role description strip (see preceding), a copy of Instructions for Playing a Role, and a copy of the Committee Meeting Problem Sheet. These five people are taken to an area outside the hearing range of the remaining group of participants. They are given five minutes to study their roles and problems independently. The facilitator instructs the role players not to reveal their hidden agendas to anyone.

II. While the committee members are studying their roles, the facilitator chooses five participants to be observers of role players. Each observer is assigned to observe a specific role player. The facilitator distributes Committee Meeting Problem Sheets and Committee Meeting Role-Play Observation Sheets to them.

III. The remaining participants are designated as group-process observers. They receive Committee Meeting Problem Sheets and Committee Meeting Process Observation Sheets.

IV. The role-player observers and the group-process observers are seated as suggested in *Physical Setting*.

V. Then the role players take their places. They are instructed by the facilitator to introduce themselves by their new names and titles only. They are told that the other participants are observers. The group of role players begins the meeting under the chairmanship of Marvin Turner.

VI. After fifteen minutes the role playing is terminated, regardless of whether the group has completed the task.

Structured Experience 9

VII. The group-process observers are asked to report.

VIII. The role-player observers are asked to report.

IX. The facilitator asks the role players to read their roles aloud to the group. Jack Simon reports last.

X. The facilitator informs the group that the purpose of this activity was to demonstrate that "what goes on underneath the table" interferes with task accomplishment. He leads a discussion of the effects of hidden agendas. The following questions may be discussed.

   1. How do hidden agendas affect group problem-solving?

   2. How do they affect the participation of individual members?

   3. What are some indications that group members have hidden agendas?

   4. When is it appropriate for group members to acknowledge their hidden agendas?

Variations

I. The content of the exercise can be adapted to local issues. Other committees—such as a student council awards committee, a task force of middle management charged with recommending personnel policy changes, or a vestry committee—can be simulated.

II. Role players can be seated as a panel in front of all of the other participants.

III. The task of the committee can be made more complex.

IV. Two rounds of the committee meeting can be held, with observers' reports after each.

Similar Structured Experiences: *Vol. I:* Structured Experience **6, 12;** *Vol. II:* **31, 41;** *Vol. III:* **73;** *'72 Annual:* **80;** *'73 Annual:* **98;** *Vol. IV:* **117.**
Lecturette Sources: *'72 Annual:* "Openness, Collusion, and Feedback"; *'73 Annual:* "Conditions Which Hinder Effective Communication."

This structured experience is based on materials developed by Jerry Gold, City College of New York. Len Miller, University of Iowa, Iowa City, assisted in developing the role descriptions.

Notes on the use of "Committee Meeting":

COMMITTEE MEETING PROBLEM SHEET
FACT-FINDING COMMITTEE OF THE CAA ADVISORY BOARD

Participants

1. Marvin Turner, shoe-store owner and operator
2. Roberta Stevens, mother of five, on welfare
3. Louis Haber, dentist
4. Jack Simon, Chamber of Commerce vice-president
5. Carol Stone, social worker, Department of Welfare

Problem

You are at a meeting of a special fact-finding committee of the Community Action Agency (CAA) Advisory Board. Your committee was established to study the suggestion that the CAA revise its procedure for electing representatives from poverty groups to the Advisory Board. At present, representatives are selected for three years, through a general, area-wide election. Your group has been authorized to come up with specific recommendations for the Board to act upon at its next meeting. The Board has advised your committee to consider two points:

1. What would be the best procedure for selecting poverty representatives?

    a. The present system (general, area-wide election) should be maintained.

    b. District elections should be held.

    c. Neighborhood elections should be held.

2. How long should the term of office be?

    a. The present term should be maintained.

    b. The representatives should serve for one year.

The chairman of the committee is Marvin Turner, who will report your recommendations to the Board.

COMMITTEE MEETING
INSTRUCTIONS FOR PLAYING A ROLE

1. Do not disclose your role description.
2. Read your description carefully and play the role conscientiously.
3. Put yourself into the role that you are given, but do not overact.
4. Be natural, but emphasize behavior aimed at fulfilling your role.

COMMITTEE MEETING ROLE BRIEFING SHEET

Carol Stone

You are a social worker with the Department of Welfare, and you would like some of your welfare clients to become active in the CAA. You think that if you help some of your clients get on the Board, this will impress your department head and you can achieve more power in the CAA program. Since your work area covers a district, you want the district form of election to be recommended. You prefer that the term of office be three years.

Marvin Turner

You are a shoe-store owner and operator, and you are an ambitious community leader. You want the poverty representatives on the Board to show a lack of unity and goals, so that the professional and governmental members can run things their way. You think that poor people are just "lazy." You support general election procedures for the whole area. This should result in electing more representatives who do not have support from a specific group of people in a small area and who do not have many specific goals in mind. You also support one-year terms to get as little continuity among members from poverty as possible.

Structured Experience 9

Roberta Stevens

You are a mother of five, receiving welfare payments for child support. You want a greater role for poverty representatives on the Board. You would also like different people from poverty to have a chance to get on the Board. You support the concept of neighborhood or small-unit elections for one-year terms. You also want more representatives from poverty on the Board than there currently are, to counteract some of the professional, governmental members.

Louis Haber

You are a dentist and you are on the City Council. You think that local government leaders as well as professional people "who know what they are doing" should have a larger say on the CAA Board. Therefore, you want a weaker voice from the poverty representatives. You support general area elections for one-year terms.

Jack Simon

You are vice-president of the Chamber of Commerce, and you are not really concerned with the work of the committee. You joined for only one reason, to meet Carol Stone and eventually ask her for a date. During the meeting you plan to agree with, and support, every point that Carol makes. Your behavior is guided by your desire to impress Carol Stone.

COMMITTEE MEETING ROLE-PLAY OBSERVATION SHEET

1. How active was the committee member whom you observed?

2. How committed was the member to the task of the group?

3. How effective was the member as a listener?

4. To what degree did the member seem motivated by personal concerns?

5. What approach did the member take in attempting to influence the group?

Structured Experience 9

COMMITTEE MEETING PROCESS OBSERVATION SHEET

Atmosphere

1. To what degree were committee members cooperating with each other?

2. What was the feeling tone of the meeting at various stages?

Participation

3. Who were the high and low participators?

4. What was the relationship between level of participation and the accomplishment of the task?

Commitment

5. To what degree were members committed to a common goal?

6. What motives did you infer for each of the members?

10. PROCESS OBSERVATION: A GUIDE

Goals

    I. To provide feedback to a group concerning its process.

    II. To provide experience for group members in observing process variables in group meetings.

Materials

Copies of the Process Observation Report Form.

Process

Participants take turns as process observers, a different observer for each meeting. The observer does not participate in the meeting but records his impressions on the Process Observation Report Form. At the end of the meeting, the observer makes an oral report of his observations, and his report is discussed. It is helpful for the first observer to have had some experience at such observation and for participants to have copies of the form while he is reporting.

Variations

    I. Sections of the observation form can be assigned to different participants in advance of the meeting.

    II. Two observers can be used instead of one, to check accuracy of observations.

    III. The meeting can be videotaped, and the entire group can use the form to analyze the process.

    IV. The observer can participate in the meeting while he is observing.

Similar Structured Experiences: *Vol. I:* Structured Experience **6;** *Vol. II:* **37, 38, 39;** *Vol. III:* **55;** *'72 Annual:* **79;** *'73 Annual:* **92.**
Lecturette Source: *'73 Annual:* "A Model of Group Development."

Notes on the use of "Process Observation":

PROCESS OBSERVATION REPORT FORM

Group_____   Date_____

Interpersonal Communication Skills

    1. Expressing (verbal and nonverbal)

    2. Listening

    3. Responding

Communication Pattern

    4. Directionality (one-to-one, one-to-group, all through a leader)

    5. Content (cognitive, affective)

Leadership

    6. Major roles (record names of participants)

_____ Information-processor		_____ Follower
_____ Coordinator		_____ Blocker
_____ Evaluator		_____ Recognition-seeker
_____ Harmonizer		_____ Dominator
_____ Gatekeeper		_____ Avoider

    7. Leadership style

      _____ Democratic   _____ Autocratic   _____ Laissez-faire

    8. Response to leadership style

      _____ Eager participation _____ Low commitment _____ Resisting

      _____ Lack of enthusiasm _____ Holding back

Structured Experience 10

Climate

    9. Feeling tone of the meeting

   10. Cohesiveness

Goals

   11. Explicitness

   12. Commitment to agreed-upon goals

Situational Variables

   13. Group size

   14. Time limit

   15. Physical facilities

Group Development

   16. State of development

   17. Rate of development

Observer Reaction

   18. Feelings experienced during the observation

   19. Feelings "here and now"

   20. Hunches, speculations, and ideas about the process observed

11. TOP PROBLEMS:
A CONSENSUS-SEEKING TASK

Goals

I. To compare the results of individual decision-making with the results of group decision-making.

II. To teach effective consensus-seeking behaviors in task groups.

Group Size

Between five and twelve participants. Several groups may be directed simultaneously. (Smaller groups tend to be more effective.)

Time Required

Approximately one-and-a-half hours.

Materials

I. Pencils.

II. A copy of the Top Problems Individual Worksheet for each participant.

III. A copy of the Top Problems Group Worksheet for each group.

Physical Setting

Participants should be seated around a square or round table during the group task phase. One dynamic that may emerge with a group seated at a rectangular table is too much control accruing to persons seated at the ends.

Process

I. After explaining the goals of the activity, the facilitator distributes copies of the Top Problems Individual Worksheet and indicates that the ranking task should take no more than fifteen minutes.

II. Then groups are formed. One copy of the Top Problems Group Worksheet is given to each group and a member is designated to record group consensus on this sheet. Individuals are instructed *not* to change any answers.

III. After about thirty minutes of group work, the facilitator explains the scoring procedure. He announces (or posts) the "correct" ranking, and each participant scores his own worksheet by adding the differences between each of his rank numbers and the correct rank number for the same item. (Make all differences positive and sum them, disregarding whether the difference is a plus or minus one.) Low scores, of course, are better than high ones. The "correct" ranking numbers follow (the ranking according to fifty leading persons polled):

1. Crime and lack of respect for law.

2. Inflation.

3. Pollution of air and water.

4. Racial tensions.

5. Drug addiction.

6. Overpopulation.

7. Unemployment.

8. Low productivity standards.

9. Labor-management disputes.

10. Inadequate housing.

11. Government reform.

12. Low educational standards.

13. Disease and poor health conditions.

IV. Each group selects one member to compute the score for the consensus rank and one member to determine the average and range of individual scores. These statistics are posted for all groups in a chart such as the following:

Outcome	Group I	Group II	Group III
Range of Individual Scores			
Average of Individual Scores			
Score for Group Consensus			

V. Groups discuss their consensus-seeking process and outcomes. The focus should be on behaviors that help or hinder group productivity.

VI. The facilitator leads a discussion of the process and outcomes in the total group. Applications of the technique are solicited. This processing may include a discussion of leadership, compromise, decision-making strategies, psychological climate, and roles.

Variations

I. Some of these worksheets may contain cultural biases, and editing of the contents may be required.

II. Ranking forms can be developed readily both prior to the training session and during the event. For example, a list of top problems facing the organization can be written. This list can be rank-ordered by a random sample of members of the organization, and their responses can be tallied to develop an answer key. Also, within the training session, a list of items can be developed by participants to generate the content of a ranking task. A survey of all participants can be conducted to develop a set of "right" answers.

III. Groups can be encouraged to experiment with alternatives to formal voting procedures: seating themselves in the order of the way they ranked a given item as individuals, rating their agreement with each item, distributing points among alternatives, etc.

IV. The group-on-group design (*Vol. I:* Structured Experience 6) can be used to heighten participation for consensus-seeking. Two rounds can be used, with two different ranking tasks.

V. The facilitator can experiment with various group sizes. Persons can be randomly assigned to groups and given a time limit for the consensus-seeking phase. They can be asked to rate their satisfaction with the outcomes before the scoring step is begun. Average satisfaction ratings can be compared across groups and can be discussed in relation to other statistical outcomes.

VI. Similar experiments can be devised to vary time limits for the consensus-seeking phase. For example, one group can be given twenty minutes, another thirty minutes, and one no limit. Satisfaction data and outcomes can be compared. (A more complex design would be to study the effects of group size and time limit simultaneously as in the model on the next page. This design requires nine groups.)

Structured Experience 11

	Group Size		
Time	Small	Medium	Large
Brief			
Long			
No Limit			

VII. As an intergroup task, the same ranking form can be filled out by two separate groups. Then they can be instructed to try to predict the ranking of the other group. The two groups can be brought together to publish their actual rankings and sets of predictions. This activity gives each group a "mirror image" of itself and can lead to more effective communication across groups.

VIII. Participants can be asked to rank-order each other (independently) in terms of the amount of influence each had on the consensus-seeking outcomes. Then each participant derives a score for himself based on the differences between his ranking of the items and the consensus ranking. The average influence ranks and the deviation scores are then correlated or compared.

IX. Sequential consensus exercises can be used, so that groups build on the learnings of the process in the first phase. New groups can be formed for the second round. One task may have "right" answers, and the other may not. Other combinations are possible, such as having the group create its own instrument for the second phase.

X. The facilitator can save considerable group time and often considerable confusion by handing out two copies of the exercise form to each participant. The participant fills in both copies along with his group identification number before his group begins its discussion. He hands one copy in to the facilitator and keeps the other for his group consensus discussion. While the group is involved in developing a consensus ranking, the facilitator may find the range of individual scores and the average of individual scores. This works particularly well if there are a number of staff so that the task goes very quickly. A chart with all the results may be made up to be shared with all the groups upon the completion of their group processing.

Submitted by John J. Sherwood, Purdue University, West Lafayette, Indiana.

Similar Structured Experiences: *Vol. II:* Structured Experience **30;** *Vol. III:* **64, 69;** *'72 Annual:* **77;** *Vol. IV:* **115.**
Lecturette Source: *'73 Annual:* "Synergy and Consensus-Seeking."

Notes on "Top Problems":

TOP PROBLEMS INDIVIDUAL WORKSHEET

In 1971, a poll was taken among a random sample of fifty leading persons in the United States who were included in the *International Yearbook* and *Statesmen's Who's Who*. (These publications list leading scientists, statesmen, jurists, business executives, publishers, and leaders in other fields.) Each leader was asked to choose the five most urgent problems facing the nation and then to rank them in order of importance.

Below is a list of the top thirteen problems facing the United States according to that poll. Your task is to rank these problems in the same order of importance as the sample of fifty leading persons did. Write the number 1 by the problem that you think was ranked as the most important; place the number 2 by the second most important problem, and so on through the number 13, which is your estimate of what was considered to be the item ranked as the least important of the problems.

_____ Low productivity standards

_____ Pollution of air and water

_____ Overpopulation

_____ Unemployment

_____ Drug addiction

_____ Disease and poor health conditions

_____ Labor-management disputes

_____ Crime and lack of respect for law

_____ Racial tensions

_____ Government reform

_____ Inadequate housing

_____ Inflation

_____ Low educational standards

TOP PROBLEMS GROUP WORKSHEET

This is an exercise in group decision-making. Your group is to employ the method of *group consensus* in reaching its decision. This means that the estimate of the ranking for each of the thirteen problems facing the United States *must* be agreed upon by each group member before it becomes a part of the group decision. Not every ranking will meet with everyone's *complete* approval. Try, as a group, to make each ranking one with which *all* group members can at least *partially* agree. Some guides to use in reaching consensus are:

1. Avoid *arguing* for your own individual judgments. Approach the task on the basis of logic.

2. Avoid changing your mind only to reach agreement and to avoid conflict. Support solutions with which you are able to agree somewhat.

3. Avoid "conflict-reducing" techniques such as majority vote, averaging, or trading in reaching your decision.

4. View differences of opinion as a help rather than a hindrance in decision-making.

_____ Low productivity standards

_____ Pollution of air and water

_____ Overpopulation

_____ Unemployment

_____ Drug addiction

_____ Disease and poor health conditions

_____ Labor-management disputes

_____ Crime and lack of respect for law

_____ Racial tensions

_____ Government reform

_____ Inadequate housing

_____ Inflation

_____ Low educational standards

Structured Experience 11

12. CHOOSING A COLOR: A MULTIPLE-ROLE-PLAY

Goals

I. To explore behavioral responses to an ambiguous task.

II. To demonstrate the effects of shared leadership.

Group Size

Seven to ten participants. Several groups may be directed simultaneously.

Time Required

Approximately forty-five minutes.

Materials

I. Prepare the following according to the Choosing a Color Envelopes Instruction Sheet:

    1. Envelope I: Directions for Phase I and seven to ten smaller envelopes, each containing an instruction card for an individual role player.

    2. Envelope II: directions for Phase II.

    3. Envelope III: directions for Phase III.

II. Large envelope containing envelopes I, II, and III.

Physical Setting

Each group is seated in a circle.

Process

I. The facilitator discusses the concept of shared leadership. The following roles are explained:

    1. Information-seeker

    2. Tension-reliever

    3. Clarifier

    4. Gatekeeper

    5. Initiator

    6. Follower

    7. Information-giver

    8. Harmonizer

II. The facilitator places the large envelope which contains Envelopes I, II, and III in the center of the group. He gives the group *no further instructions or information*. (The group must complete Phases I, II, and III by following directions in the envelopes.)

III. After Phase III has been completed, the facilitator leads a discussion of the entire process, with special focus on the dimensions of shared leadership.

Variations

I. The content of the exercise can be adapted to the particular learning needs of participants by changing the nature of the problem and the positions which role players are to take. For example, the adaptation called Bus Duty was developed for use within an education setting. (Robert T. Williams, Colorado State University, Fort Collins.) The Instruction Sheet for Bus Duty follows at the end of this section.

II. The task can be made less ambiguous by instructing the group concerning step-by-step procedures.

III. After the problem has been solved, role players (and observers) can write down their role nominations as the beginning of the processing stage.

Similar Structured Experiences: *Vol. I:* Structured Experience **6, 9;** *Vol. II:* **31, 38, 41;** *Vol. III:* **73;** *'72 Annual:* **80;** *'73 Annual:* **98;** *Vol. IV:* **117.**

Submitted by J. William Pfeiffer, University Associates, San Diego, California.

Structured Experience 12

Notes on the use of "Choosing a Color":

CHOOSING A COLOR ENVELOPES INSTRUCTION SHEET

The following instructions are written on the large envelope which contains envelopes I, II, and III.

Instructions: Enclosed you will find three envelopes which contain directions for the phases of this group session. You are to open the envelope labeled I at once. Subsequent instructions will tell you when to open Envelope II and Envelope III.

Envelope I holds a sheet of paper with the following group task instructions and smaller envelopes each containing a role-player card.

Instructions for Group Task: Phase I

Time Allowed: Fifteen minutes.

Task: The group is to choose a color.

Special Instructions: Each member is to take one of the smaller envelopes from Envelope I and to follow the individual instructions contained on the card in it.

Do not let anyone else see your instructions!

(After fifteen minutes go on to the next envelope.)

Instructions for Facilitator: How to Prepare Role-Player Cards.

Envelope I holds smaller envelopes containing instructions for roles and positions that role players are to take. (Two of the instructions include special knowledge.) If there are fewer than ten participants in the group, eliminate as many of the *last three* roles and positions as are necessary. There must be at least seven people in the group. The information should be typed on cards. Then each card should be put in a small envelope.

Structured Experience 12

1.

Role: Information-seeker

Position: Support blue.

2.

Role: Tension-reliever

Position: Introduce the idea of a different color—orange.

3.

Role: Clarifier

Position: Support red.

4.

Role: None

Position: None

(You have the special knowledge that the group is going to be asked to select a chairman later in the exercise. You are to conduct yourself in such a manner that they will select you as chairman.)

5.

Role: Gatekeeper

Position: Against red.

6.

Role: Initiator

Position: Support green.

7.

Role: None

Position: None

(You have the special knowledge that the group is going to be asked to select a chairman later in the exercise. You are to conduct yourself in such a manner that they will select you as chairman.)

8.

Role: Follower

Position: Against red.

9.

Role: Information-giver

Position: Against blue.

10.

Role: Harmonizer

Position: Against green

Envelope II contains a sheet of paper with the following instructions.

Instructions for Group Task: Phase II

Time Allowed: Five minutes.

Task: You are to choose a group chairman.
(After the chairman is chosen, go on to the next envelope.)

Envelope III contains a sheet of paper with the following instructions.

Instructions for Group Task: Phase III.

Time Allowed: Ten minutes.

Task: You are to discuss the process that emerged during the problem-solving phase of this group session.

Special Instructions: The chairman will lead this discussion. Sample questions:
1. What behaviors helped the group in accomplishing its task?
2. What behaviors hindered the group in accomplishing its task?
(After ten minutes return the materials to their respective envelopes.)

INSTRUCTION SHEET FOR BUS DUTY: A MULTIPLE-ROLE-PLAY
(Variation I to "Choosing a Color")

Situation and Task: You are a member of a group of elementary school teachers on "bus duty" one Friday afternoon. When the buses arrive to pick up the children, your group is informed that one bus is out of service. Therefore, thirty-nine students must wait for forty-five minutes while one bus makes its run and returns.

Your principal has left the building. Your group must decide what to do. It is beginning to rain.

1.

Role: Initiator

Position: We should call the principal for directions.

2.

Role: Clarifier

Position: We should call parents to pick up children; teachers should leave.

3.

Role: Informer

Position: Take the children into the multi-purpose room to wait. All teachers should stay until the bus returns.

4.

Role: Compromiser

Position: Teachers should stay until the bus returns.

Structured Experience 12

5.

Role: Aggressor

Position: School is over for the day; teachers should leave.

6.

Role: Avoider

Position: We should crowd the children on the available buses.

7.

Role: None

Position: None

(You have special knowledge that the group is going to be asked to select a chairman later in the exercise; you are to conduct yourself in such a manner that they will select you as chairman.)

8.

Role: None

Position: None

(You have special knowledge that the group is going to be asked to select a chairman later in the exercise; you are to conduct yourself in such a manner that they will select you as chairman.)

9.

Role: Encourager

Position: Support teachers staying with the children.

10.

Role: Gatekeeper

Position: Support teachers leaving.

13. JOHARI WINDOW: AN EXPERIENCE IN SELF-DISCLOSURE AND FEEDBACK

Goals

I. To introduce the concept of the Johari Window.

II. To permit participants to process data about themselves in terms of self-disclosure and feedback.

Group Size

Eight to twelve. Several groups may be directed simultaneously.

Time Required

Approximately two hours.

Materials

I. Newsprint and felt-tipped marker.

II. Copies of the Johari Window Self-Knowledge and Recording Sheet for all participants.

III. Copies of the Johari Window Feedback Sheet for all participants.

IV. Pencils for all participants.

Physical Setting

Circle of chairs.

Process

I. The facilitator presents a lecturette on the Johari Window* concept. (The name Johari refers to the originators, Joe Luft and Harry Ingham.) He displays the chart on newsprint and discusses the four "windows."

---

*Reprinted from *Group Processes: An Introduction to Group Dynamics* (1970) by Joseph Luft, by permission of National Press Books. Copyright © 1963, 1970 by Joseph Luft.

	Known to Self	Not Known to Self
Known to Others	I. Area of Free Activity (Public Self)	II. Blind Area ("Bad-Breath" Area)
Not Known to Others	III. Avoided or Hidden Area (Private Self)	IV. Area of Unknown Activity

The following charts illustrate the effects of self-disclosure and feedback.
Under conditions of self-disclosure:

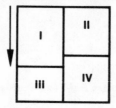

Under conditions of feedback:

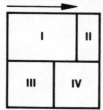

Under conditions of self-disclosure and feedback:

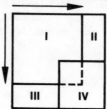

II. Participants complete Part I of the Johari Window Self-Knowledge and Recording Sheet.

III. Participants fill out the Johari Window Feedback Sheet.

IV. The facilitator collects the Feedback Sheets and reads them aloud anonymously. Participants record perceptions held of them on the Self-Knowledge and Recording Sheet, which they keep. This provides data on Area II, the blind area, and permits the participant to test whether he has actually revealed any hidden data about himself earlier in the group's life.

V. Group members discuss their reactions to the feedback received and to the concept of the Johari Window.

Variations

I. Instead of collecting the Feedback Sheets, the facilitator can instruct participants to read them aloud, in turn.

II. Each participant can receive his feedback all at one time rather than interspersed with others. He is helped immediately afterward to process the data in terms of ways in which he sees himself.

III. The Feedback Sheet can be cut into strips, to be distributed by participants to each other. These may be signed or anonymous.

Similar Structured Experiences: *Vol I:* Structured Experience **17, 18, 23;** *Vol. II:* **38, 42, 57, 58;** *'73 Annual:* **97, 99;** *Vol. IV:* **104, 107, 122.**
Lecturette Sources: *'72 Annual:* "Openness, Collusion, and Feedback"; *'73 Annual:* "Johari Window."

Notes on the use of "Johari Window":

JOHARI WINDOW SELF-KNOWLEDGE AND RECORDING SHEET

Instructions

I. List in the left column below the major assets and liabilities of your personality. Then place a check mark in front of those aspects which you have revealed so far to participants. (Use the Feedback Sheet to write your impressions of other participants.)

II. When the facilitator collects the Feedback Sheets and reads them aloud, use the right column of this sheet to record perceptions of you held by other participants. This sheet is yours to keep.

Assets Self-Perceptions	**Assets** Others' Perceptions
Liabilities Self-Perceptions	**Liabilities** Others' Perceptions

JOHARI WINDOW FEEDBACK SHEET

Instructions: Write your impressions of the major assets and liabilities of each participant, including yourself, in the spaces below. These will be read aloud anonymously
as feedback.

Participant	Assets	Liabilities
_____	_____	_____
_____	_____	_____
_____	_____	_____
_____	_____	_____
_____	_____	_____
_____	_____	_____
_____	_____	_____
_____	_____	_____
_____	_____	_____
_____	_____	_____
_____	_____	_____

Structured Experience 13

14. CONFLICT RESOLUTION: A COLLECTION OF TASKS

Below are listed several activities that can be used to generate data about how groups resolve conflict. It is important that the facilitator be sensitive to the amount of data that can emerge and that he allow adequate processing time.

1. *Lineup.* Participants are instructed to position themselves in the order of their influence in the group. The person at the head of the line is the most influential. Staff may be included. The task may be carried out nonverbally. Other traits besides influence (supportiveness, risk-taking, verbosity) can be used.

2. *Rating Leadership.* Within a strict time limit, participants develop a rating scale on dimensions of leadership and rate each other.

3. *Choosing a Family.* Each participant chooses a family from among the other group members and explains the reasons for his choices.

4. *Ambiguity.* An unstructured situation is set up by directions such as the following: "During the next thirty minutes the task of the group is to decide how it wants to spend its time."

5. *Elimination.* Each group member nominates one other person to be eliminated from the group.

6. *Similarities.* Participants develop a list of all possible pairs of group members and rank-order them on similarity.

7. *Kelly's Triangle.* Participants develop a list of all possible triads in the group. Within each triad, two persons are to be designated similar to each other and different from the third.

8. *Role Reversal.* The facilitator introduces a controversial subject, such as women's liberation, sexual freedom, or capital punishment. Each participant briefly expresses his position. Then the group discusses the subject, with each person arguing the point of view opposite to his own expressed position.

9. *Subgrouping.* The group is divided into two or more subgroups on the basis of predominant characteristics. Criteria could include sex, age, degree of participation, or political persuasion. Subgroups confront each other.

Similar Structured Experiences: *Vol. II:* Structured Experience 43; *Vol. III:* 56; '72 Annual: **75;** '73 Annual: **94, 95;** *Vol. IV:* **109, 123.**
Lecturette Sources: '72 Annual: "Transcendence Theory," "Notes on Freedom"; '73 Annual: "Confrontation: Types, Conditions, and Outcomes."

Notes on the use of "Conflict Resolution":

15. RESIDENCE HALLS: A CONSENSUS-SEEKING TASK

Goals

I. To study the degree to which members of a group agree on certain values.

II. To assess the decision-making norms of the group.

III. To identify the "natural leadership" functioning in the group.

Group Size

Between five and twelve participants. Several groups may be directed simultaneously in the same room. (Synergistic outcomes are more likely to be achieved by smaller groups, *i.e.*, five to seven participants.)

Time Required

Approximately one hour.

Materials

I. Copies of the Residence Halls Ranking Sheet for all participants.

II. Pencils for all participants.

Physical Setting

It is desirable to have small groups seated around tables and to have the groups far enough apart so as not to disturb each other. Lapboards or desk chairs may be utilized instead of tables.

Process

I. The facilitator forms groups and announces that they will engage in an activity to accomplish the goals spelled out above.

II. He distributes copies of the Residence Halls Ranking Sheet. The facilitator functions as a timekeeper according to the schedule on the sheet. One or more members may function as process observers. (See "Process Observation," *Vol. I*: Structured Experience 10.)

III. After the allotted time, the group discusses the process in terms of stated goals

Variations

I. The ranking sheet can be easily revised to fit situations other than residence halls. The content may be the goals of the organization or group, characteristics of an ideal leader, desirable characteristics of teachers (principals, ministers, counselors, supervisors, employers, etc.), or any other relevant list. One suggestion might be to conduct a problem census of the organization or group and to use that list as the items to be rank-ordered.

II. When several groups in the same organization (class, institution, etc.) engage in this experience simultaneously, it is sometimes helpful to summarize the rank orders for the several groups and to have a discussion of the agreements and disagreements among the groups.

Similar Structured Experiences: *Vol. I:* Structured Experience 11; *Vol. II:* **30**; *Vol. III:* **64, 69**; *'72 Annual:* **77**; *Vol. IV:* **115**.
Lecturette Sources: *'73 Annual:* "Synergy and Consensus-Seeking," "Value Clarification."

Notes on the use of "Residence Halls":

RESIDENCE HALLS RANKING SHEET

Rank the following functions of the residence-hall system according to the importance *you* attach to them. Write the number 1 in front of the most important, the number 2 before the second most important, etc. You have ten minutes for this task.

After members of your group have finished working individually, arrive at a rank ordering *as a group*. The group has thirty minutes for the task. Do *not* choose a formal leader.

Individual Rank	Group Rank	
————	————	Residence halls exist to help college students develop social maturity.
————	————	Residence-hall organizations should militate for improving the quality of student life.
————	————	The residence hall is where students develop business and social contacts that will be helpful after graduation.
————	————	Residence halls provide a "home away from home" where the resident is accepted and wanted.
————	————	The residence-hall system encourages worthwhile fellowship.
————	————	The residence hall is an experiment in living, through which the student comes to know his prejudices and tries to overcome them.
————	————	Participation in residence-hall activities is training for leadership in adult life.
————	————	Residence halls support and enhance the classroom learning experience of students.
————	————	In the residence-hall system, students are treated as adults, not as adolescents who need to be controlled.
————	————	Residence halls function as laboratories for democratic action.

16. FANTASIES: SUGGESTIONS FOR INDIVIDUALS AND GROUPS

Fantasy techniques are often used in human relations training to promote heightened awareness of self and others. However, these methods are somewhat controversial, and care should be exercised in their use. It is important for the facilitator to make the following considerations:

Goals   Fantasy exercises should be clearly related to the goals of the training. They should not simply be isolated events.

Affect   Occasionally fantasy techniques generate a heightened feeling response, which can be modulated somewhat by facilitator interventions.

Processing   It is necessary for the data that are brought into focus by the use of fantasy methods to be adequately processed.

Voluntariness Participants should not be coerced (either by the facilitator or by the group) into revealing data about themselves.

Non-Response Sometimes participants are unable to create fantasy material. These "non-responses" should be accepted as legitimate data.

Theory   The facilitator should be prepared to justify his use of fantasy exercises in terms of a well-integrated theory of learning.

Individual Fantasies

These are suggestions for fantasies that group participants may create individually. The fantasies may be made in the group session, to be shared later with partners or with the entire group. Typically the facilitator announces that group participants close their eyes and develop a daydream for two or three minutes. After a brief period of silence for relaxation (quiet music helps), the facilitator "sets up" the beginning of the fantasy. Innumerable situations are possible. Here are a few:

1. Locate yourself in some place. Now listen. Someone is calling your name.

2. Imagine yourself somewhere and the rest of the group coming towards you.

3. In a few minutes we will need a volunteer to be the focus of attention in the group. Imagine that right now there are two people in your head debating about whether you should volunteer. One says you should, one says you should not. Watch them and listen to them. Let them arrive at some conclusion.

4. Make yourself tiny and enter your own body. Be as aware as you can of what you see and how you feel. Inventory each of your senses as you move about within your body.

5. Think of yourself as being at a spot hundreds of miles away from any form of civilization. How do you feel? What do you see? What do you do?

6. You are standing in front of a cave on the side of a mountain. Go in.

7. You are with some participant of this group, and the two of you are walking through a city park.

8. If you could be anything other than a person, what would you be?

Guided Individual Fantasies

Some group participants experience difficulty in developing fantasies and may express anxiety about inability to fantasize "on cue." Sometimes it is useful for the facilitator to help a group member to fantasize by asking him to close his eyes and create a story out loud. When blockages occur, the facilitator may help by using such suggestions as: "What are you seeing right now?" "How are you feeling?" "Can you smell anything?" "Move in a little closer." "What do you want to do right now? Do it."

Guided fantasies tend to be more emotional experiences than individual fantasies. The facilitator should be prepared to help the group member deal with feelings elicited.

Here are some suggested situations.

9. You are walking down a road that is bordered by a high brick wall. You come to a heavy iron gate that is slightly ajar. You go through the gate.

10. You are at the end of a very long culvert. You look in and you cannot see the end— it is dark inside. You stoop down and begin to crawl into the pipe.

11. You are sitting alone in your living room in the middle of an autumn afternoon. Someone is knocking at the door.

12. You are all alone on a deserted ocean beach. It is dark, and it is becoming chilly. You are digging for clams, and you have a bucket full of them which you are going to take home.

13. You are sitting in a college classroom hearing a boring lecture with three hundred other students. For some unknown reason you have the strong impulse to tell the professor that he is wasting your time. With some effort you stand up.

Facilitator-Structured Fantasies

The following two activities are examples of fantasies directed by the facilitator. Both are best conducted by having participants lie on the floor. Subgroups can be formed immediately afterwards for processing.

14. Imagine yourself inside a cocoon. Feel the inside of the cocoon. Slowly explore your space inside the cocoon. How do you feel? Now slowly get out of the cocoon and be aware of your senses.

15. Think of yourself as a puppet, with strings attached to parts of your body. The puppeteer slowly raises your left hand—up, up, up, and holds it there. Then he suddenly lets it drop! Then he lifts your right hand—up, up, up, and holds it there. Then he lets it drop! He slowly lifts your left leg, etc.

Group Fantasies

Three major variations of group fantasies are common.

16. Everyone sits in a circle with eyes closed. Someone begins a fantasy involving the entire group. Members contribute to the story as they feel a part of it.

17. One member lies on the floor and begins a fantasy. Other participants are free to join him on the floor, to become a part of the fantasy, and to contribute to it. Individuals may leave the fantasy by getting up from the floor.

18. Group members lie on the floor with their heads together, their bodies forming the spokes of a wheel. In this way, whispers can be heard by all. Someone begins a fantasy, either alone or involving one or more other group participants, and others contribute as they identify with the story.

Most of the suggestions for individual fantasies would be appropriate for group fantasy. Any participant should feel free to suggest that the fantasy be terminated. Later discussion might center around such dimensions as fantasy content, group cohesiveness, tensions and subgroupings within the group, feelings experienced, and roles participants played in the story.

Similar Structured Experiences: *'72 Annual:* Structured Experience **85;** *'73 Annual:* **89;** *Vol. IV:* **119.**
Lecturette Source: *'72 Annual:* "Communication Modes: An Experiential Lecture."

Notes on the use of "Fantasies":

17. LEVELING: GIVING AND RECEIVING ADVERSE FEEDBACK

Goals

I. To let participants compare their perceptions of how a group sees them with the actual feedback obtained from the group.

II. To legitimize giving negative feedback within a group.

III. To develop skills in giving negative feedback.

Group Size

Eight to twelve participants.

Time Required

Approximately ten minutes per participant.

Materials

Paper and pencil for each participant.

Physical Setting

I. Participants are seated in a circle for the first phase.

II. Participants are seated in a semicircle, with one chair "on stage" facing the semicircle, for the second phase.

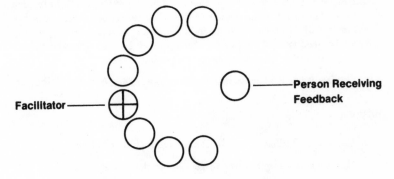

Process

I. The facilitator discusses the goals of the exercise.

II. Paper and pencils are distributed, and participants are instructed to write down the first names of all group members. This list should begin with the facilitator and proceed clockwise. Names should be written down the left-hand side of the paper, with a space between each name.

III. Individuals are instructed to write a short piece of adverse feedback about each participant, including the facilitator and himself. The facilitator points out the following:

1. Feedback will be given anonymously.

2. The feedback should consist of a list of three to five adjectives rather than a sentence.

3. Each participant *must* comment on every other participant.

4. This task should take about fifteen minutes.

IV. The papers are collected by the facilitator.

V. For the second phase of the exercise, chairs are rearranged according to the diagram in *Physical Setting*.

VI. If there are no volunteers to be the first to receive feedback, the facilitator designates one member.

VII. The format for this phase is divided into four parts.

Part one consists of each individual anticipating adverse feedback he expects to receive and telling the group about it briefly.

Part two consists of reading the comments about an individual.

Part three consists of the individual comparing the degree of agreement between anticipated perception and actual perception.

Part four consists of exploring the individual's feeling reactions to adverse feedback. (The group in the semicircle should be asked not to react, either verbally or nonverbally, to the person receiving feedback at this time, to prevent an overload of feedback.) Each person who has received feedback chooses his successor to go "on stage," and the process is repeated.

VIII. The facilitator leads a discussion about the exercise, focusing on the stated goals.

Variations

I. Content of feedback could be changed to include positive data.

II. Feedback can be given face-to-face rather than anonymously.

III. The feedback sheet could be cut into strips and distributed by participants to each other. Strips may be taped onto a sheet of newsprint to make a poster for each participant. (One poster is made at a time.)

IV. The individual being focused on may leave the room while the rest attempt to reach consensus about his adverse feedback. (This heightens the possibility that feedback will be honest and straightforward.)

Similar Structured Experiences: *Vol I:* Structured Experience **13, 18, 23;** *Vol. II:* **42;** *Vol. III:* **57, 58;** *'73 Annual:* **97;** *Vol. IV:* **104, 107.**
Lecturette Sources: *'72 Annual:* "Openness, Collusion, and Feedback"; *'73 Annual:* "Johari Window," "Confrontation: Types, Conditions, and Outcomes."

Notes on the use of "Leveling":

Submitted by J. William Pfeiffer, University Associates, San Diego, California.

Structured Experience 17

18. DEPENDENCY-INTIMACY: A FEEDBACK EXPERIENCE

Goals

I. To provide instrumented feedback.

II. To study how the personal dimensions of dependency and intimacy affect group development.

Group Size

Eight to twelve participants.

Time Required

Approximately one-and-a-half hours.

Materials

I. Copies of the Dependency-Intimacy Rating Form for all participants.

II. Copies of the Dependency-Intimacy Tally Form for all participants.

III. Pencils for all participants.

Physical Setting

Participants should be seated comfortably for writing.

Process

I. The facilitator gives a lecturette on the relationship between group participants' personalities and group development. He stresses the centrality of the dimensions of dependency (orientations to authority, power, and structure) and intimacy (orientations toward closeness and personalness).

II. Participants complete the Dependency-Intimacy Rating Form anonymously.

III. The facilitator collects the completed forms and distributes tally forms.

IV. The facilitator reads the ratings aloud, and each participant tallies his own ratings. The facilitator redistributes the rating forms.

V. Participants react to their ratings—how they feel about them, how accurate they think they are. They are encouraged to solicit feedback.

VI. The group discusses its development in terms of behaviors that facilitate or impede goal attainment.

Variations

I. The ratings can be made non-anonymously.

II. Participants can rank-order members of the group on the two traits rather than rate them.

III. The tallying can be done quickly by one or two persons while the group takes a break.

IV. Tallies can be made on newsprint so that all data can be seen at one time.

V. Other traits can be used, such as those measured by *FIRO-B* (inclusion, control, and affection).

Similar Structured Experiences: *Vol. I:* Structured Experience **13, 17, 23;** *Vol. II:* **38, 42;** *Vol. III:* **57, 58, 59;** *'73 Annual:* **99;** *Vol. IV:* **104, 123.**
Lecturette Sources: *'72 Annual:* "Openness, Collusion, and Feedback"; *'73 Annual:* "Johari Window," "Dependency and Intimacy."

Notes on the use of "Dependency-Intimacy":

Submitted by John E. Jones, University Associates, San Diego, California.

Structured Experience 18

DEPENDENCY-INTIMACY RATING FORM

Instructions: Below are scales on which you are to rate yourself and all other participants on two traits—dependency and intimacy. Read descriptions of the two personality traits. In front of participants' names, write the numbers on the dependency scale corresponding to your ratings of the persons. Then record your ratings on the intimacy scale of each.

DEPENDENCY

1	2	3	4	5	6

Dependent	Independent	Counterdependent
Relies on structure, leader, group, and agenda	Feels comfortable without structure	Rebels against almost all forms of structure

INTIMACY

1	2	3	4	5	6

Overpersonal	Personal	Counterpersonal
Needs to establish close personal relations with everyone, and needs to keep the group on a personal level	Encourages and generates personal relations when they seem appropriate	Needs to keep relations with others formal and impersonal, and needs to keep group interaction formal and impersonal

Dependency	Intimacy	Group Member
_____	_____	_____
_____	_____	_____
_____	_____	_____
_____	_____	_____
_____	_____	_____
_____	_____	_____
_____	_____	_____
_____	_____	_____
_____	_____	_____

DEPENDENCY-INTIMACY TALLY FORM

Name _____

Dependency and intimacy are not seen as linear dimensions; that is, the extremes of dependency and counterdependency are dynamically close, as are overpersonalness and counterpersonalness. The person who is conflicted on either dependency or intimacy may display behaviors on both ends of the continuum. He may alternately be dependent and counterdependent in a stressful situation, even in the same group meeting. The circles below demonstrate the relationship between the extremes of these two dimensions. Tally the ratings you receive from group members by marking X's on the circles.

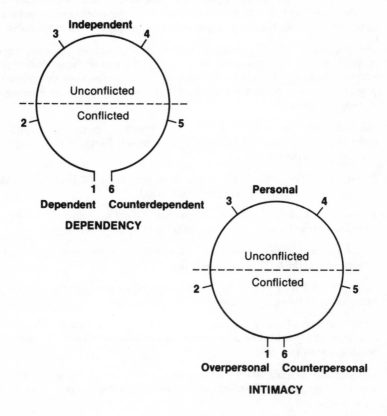

19. AWARENESS EXPANSION: A POTPOURRI

Below are listed several activities that can be useful in personal growth laboratories to heighten one's sensory awareness.

1. *Exploring Your Space.* Lie on the floor, eyes closed. With your hands explore the space you occupy. Stretch and contract your space.

2. *Pounding.* Beat vigorously on a pillow or cushion. Focus on all of the feelings elicited.

3. *Yelling.* Yell as loudly as you can any of the following: your name, the name of a significant person, how you are feeling, taboo words, numbers, nonsense syllables, or primitive sounds. Explore your physiological and psychological responses.

4. *Opening an Egg.* Without talking, explore an egg. Try to break it by squeezing on it. While paying attention to your own feelings, think of all the symbolism connected with an egg. Then open the egg in any way you feel appropriate and explore the contents. Alternative: Use an orange. Then eat the orange, focusing on its taste and textures.

5. *Deep Breathing.* Lie on the floor, eyes closed. Breathe as deeply as you can, concentrating on the effects of increased oxygen intake. Fantasize observing your breathing from the inside.

6. *Feeling Hands.* Feel your left hand with your right hand. Be aware of touching yourself. Then reverse, exploring your right hand.

7. *Pressure Points.* Mentally check over your entire body and locate all of the pressure points (your bottom, your shoes, your bra strap, your belt, etc.).

8. *Washing Hands.* "Wash" your hands with sand, salt, snow, or an ice cube. Pay attention to all the feelings you experience.

9. *Eating Bread.* Eat a piece of bread, free associating on the subject of bread while being aware of the taste and texture.

10. *Stretching.* Extend your left arm as high above your head as you can. Then extend your right arm. Stand as high on your tiptoes as you can. Then try to take up as much space as you can.

11. *Tapping and Slapping.* With your fingertips lightly tap all over your head (or a partner's head), feeling the effects of the touch. Then slap as many areas of your body as you can.

12. *Sense Census.* Lie down, eyes closed.

    a. *Feel* your space, the floor, your body (externally and internally).

    b. With eyes still closed, *hear* as much as you can right now.

c. Stand up, eyes closed. Mill about the room and *smell* as many smells as you can.

d. Sit down, eyes still closed, and *taste* a slice of lemon, lick salt from your palm, eat a carrot stick, or suck on a stick of peppermint candy.

e. Without turning your head, open your eyes and *see* as much detail in your field of vision as you can. Concentrate on how your peripheral vision operates.

f. Stand up and mill around, eyes open, being aware of as many of your senses as possible.

Similar Structured Experiences: *Vol. I:* Structured Experience **16, 20, 22;** *Vol. II:* **44, 47;** *Vol. III:* **71, 72;** *'72 Annual:* **85;** *Vol. IV:* **119.**
Lecturette Source: *'72 Annual:* "Communication Modes: An Experiential Lecture."

Notes on the use of "Awareness Expansion":

Structured Experience 19

20. GRAPHICS: SELF-DISCLOSURE ACTIVITIES

Below are listed several structured experiences that generate self-disclosure data through graphics. One advantage of these methods is that participants often can disclose themselves more quickly and straightforwardly than through verbal transactions. The facilitator should ensure that there is adequate processing time for each activity.

1. *The Road of Life.* Participants are given sheets of newsprint and felt-tipped markers. Each places a dot on the paper to represent his birth. Without lifting the marker from the paper, he portrays a series of critical incidents in his lifetime.

2. *Advertisement for Myself.* Using collage materials (such as construction paper, scissors, glue, tape, newspapers, and magazines), participants create brochures advertising themselves.

3. *Coat of Arms.* After a brief introduction to heraldry, participants create coats of arms to represent themselves.

4. *Comic Strip.* Participants are given paper and pencils and draw lines to divide the paper into twelve equal-sized sections. In each section they are to depict a significant event in which they were involved. (These may be limited to events within the group's life.)

5. *Silhouettes.* The facilitator forms dyads. Participants take turns drawing full-sized silhouettes of their partners on large sheets of paper. These drawings are posted and identified. Participants then add features that they associate with the person.

6. *The Group and I.* At the end of the first meeting of a group, the facilitator passes out newsprint and felt-tipped markers. Participants divide these papers into as many sections as there will be group sessions and post these sheets. Each participant graphically portrays on his sheet his relationship with the group after each session.

7. *Collaborative Drawing.* Dyads are given one sheet of paper and one felt-tipped marker. Without talking, they collaborate on creating a drawing.

8. *Group Collage.* Given materials such as those in item 2 above, the group creates a collage representing itself.

9. *Mural.* A large group, such as an entire laboratory community, can create a montage depicting itself. This can be made on a roll of wrapping paper using cutouts from magazines. The mural is affixed to a wall, and each participant briefly explains his contribution.

Similar Structured Experiences: *Vol. I:* Structured Experience 5; *Vol. III:* **49**; *'73 Annual:* **90**; *Vol. IV:* **120**.
Lecturette Source: *'73 Annual:* "Johari Window."

Notes on the use of "Graphics":

Structured Experience 20

21. DYADIC ENCOUNTER: A PROGRAM FOR DEVELOPING RELATIONSHIPS

Goal

To explore knowing and trusting another person through mutual self-disclosure and risk-taking.

Group Size

Any number of paired participants.

Time Required

A minimum of two hours. (May be scheduled in two sessions of one hour each.)

Materials

One Dyadic Encounter "booklet" for each participant. The booklet should be prepared in such a way that participants are presented statements one at a time. The format which follows illustrates how each page should look. (Pre-assembled, reusable Dyadic Encounter booklets may be ordered from University Associates. The price is fifty cents each; the minimum order is twelve copies.)

Physical Setting

Pairs are instructed to find a private place somewhere in the immediate vicinity, such as in other rooms or out of doors.

Process

I. The facilitator discusses how work relationships are enhanced by self-disclosure and feedback.

II. Participants are paired by any appropriate method. (Sample criteria: boss-subordinate, new-old employees, persons who do not know each other very well.)

III. A copy of the Dyadic Encounter booklet is given to each participant, and the pairs are instructed to find a private place to work. An announcement is made concerning when the total group is to reassemble.

IV. After the paired activity, the total group reassembles. The facilitator assists in processing of the event by encouraging each participant to share what he learned about *himself* through the experience. (Remember that a ground rule of confidentiality is established by the directions.)

Variations

I. The Dyadic Encounter exercise can be used in conjunction with Dialog (*Vol. IV:* Structured Experience 116). The two structured experiences can be incorporated into the same laboratory design to build on each other.

II. The event can be divided into two sessions of one hour each by stopping the discussion at number 28. The two sessions can be scheduled at different times.

III. The session can be planned to take place as the last event of the training day. Participants are instructed to spend *at least* one hour on the activity.

IV. Groups of various sizes (triads, quartets, etc.) can utilize the Dyadic Encounter booklet. This variation takes more time.

V. A family can utilize the Dyadic Encounter in a series of sessions, going through several items at a time.

VI. The Dyadic Encounter can be used to establish helping pairs that will meet several times during the training event. These persons may be paired initially on the basis of "presumed incompatibility."

VII. Items from the Dyadic Encounter booklet may be posted on newsprint to stimulate group discussion. Subgroups may be formed to exchange responses to selected items like an ice-breaking activity in a laboratory or workshop.

VIII. Since many of the Dyadic Encounter items are based on Schutz' theory of interpersonal needs, the structured experience can be used in conjunction with his *FIRO* scales.

Similar Structured Experiences: *Vol. II:* Structured Experience **25, 45;** *Vol. III:* **70;** *Vol. IV:* **116, 118.**
Lecturette Sources: *'72 Annual:* "Openness, Collusion, and Feedback"; *'73 Annual:* "Johari Window."

Submitted by John E. Jones, University Associates, San Diego, California, and Johanna J. Jones, University of Iowa, Iowa City.

Structured Experience 21

Notes on the use of "Dyadic Encounter":

DYADIC ENCOUNTER "BOOKLET" PAGES

Prepare a booklet for each participant with pages numbered as follows:

1

DYADIC ENCOUNTER: A PROGRAM FOR DEVELOPING RELATIONSHIPS

2

Read silently. Do not look ahead in this booklet.

A theme frequently thought and occasionally voiced when persons are brought together for the first time is, "I'd like to get to know you, but I don't know how." This sentiment often is expressed in encounter groups and emerges in marriage and other dyadic relationships. Getting to know another person involves a learnable set of skills and attitudes, self-disclosure, self-awareness, nonpossessive caring, risk-taking, trust, acceptance, and feedback.

In an understanding, nonevaluative atmosphere, one confides significant data about himself to another who reciprocates. This "stretching" results in a greater feeling of trust, understanding, and acceptance, and the relationship becomes closer, allowing for more significant self-disclosure and greater risk-taking. As the two continue to share their experience authentically, they come to know and trust each other in ways that may enable them to be highly resourceful to each other.

This Dyadic Encounter experience is designed to facilitate getting to know another person on a fairly intimate level. The discussion items are open-ended statements which can be completed at whatever level of self-disclosure one wishes.

Structured Experience 21

3

The following ground rules should govern this experience:

1. All of the data discussed should be kept strictly confidential.

2. Do not look ahead in the booklet.

3. One partner should initiate the encounter on even-numbered pages while the other partner initiates on odd-numbered pages, so that the same individual is not always the initiator.

4. Each partner responds to each statement before continuing. Complete statements in the order they appear. Do not skip items.

5. You may decline to answer any question asked by your partner.

6. Stop the exercise if either partner becomes uncomfortable or anxious. Either partner can stop the exchange.

Look up. If your partner has finished reading, turn the page and begin.

4

My name is . . .

5

My titles are . . .

6

My marital status is . . .

7

My hometown is . . .

8

The reason I'm here is . . .

9

Right now I'm feeling . . .

10

One of the most important skills in getting to know another person is listening. In order to get a check on your ability to understand what your partner is communicating, the two of you should go through the following steps *one at a time.*

The first speaker is to complete the following item in two or three sentences:

When I think about the future, I see myself . . .

The second speaker repeats *in his own words* what the first speaker has just said. The first speaker must be satisfied that he has been heard accurately.

The second speaker completes the same item himself in two or three sentences.

The first speaker then paraphrases what the second speaker just said, to the satisfaction of the second speaker.

11

Share what you may have learned about yourself as a listener. To check the accuracy of your listening and understanding, the two of you may find yourselves later saying to each other, "What I hear you saying is . . ."

12

When I'm in a new group, I . . .

13

When I enter a room full of people, I usually feel . . .

14

When I'm feeling anxious in a new situation, I usually . . .

Structured Experience 21

  15

In groups I feel most comfortable when the leader . . .

                                                                          16

Social norms make me feel . . .

                                                                          17

In ambiguous, unstructured situations, I . . .
Listening Check: "What I hear you saying is . . ."

                                                                          18

I'm happiest when . . .

                                                                          19

The thing that turns me on the most is . . .

                                                                          20

Look your partner in the eyes while you respond to this item.
Right now I'm feeling . . .

                                                                          21

The thing that concerns me the most about joining groups is . . .

                                                                          22

When I'm rejected, I usually . . .

                                                                          23

To me, belonging is . . .

24

A forceful leader makes me feel . . .

25

Breaking rules that seem arbitrary makes me feel . . .

26

I like to be just a follower when . . .

27

The thing that turns me off the most is . . .

28

I feel most affectionate when . . .

29

Establish eye contact and hold your partner's hand while completing this item.
Toward you right now, I feel . . .

30

When I'm alone, I usually . . .

31

In crowds I . . .

Structured Experience 21

32

In a group I usually get most involved when . . .
Listening Check: "What I hear you saying is . . ."

33

To me, taking orders from another person . . .

34

I'm rebellious when . . .

35

In a working meeting, having an agenda . . .

36

Checkup: Have a two or three-minute discussion about this experience so far. Keep eye contact as much as you can, and try to cover the following points:
    How well are you listening?
    How open and honest have you been?
    How eager are you to continue this interchange?
    How well do you feel that you are getting to know each other?

37

The emotion I find most difficult to control is . . .

38

My most frequent daydreams are about . . .

39

My weakest point is . . .

40

I love . . .

41

I feel jealous about . . .

42

Right now I'm feeling . . .

43

I'm afraid of . . .

44

I believe in . . .

45

I'm most ashamed of . . .

46

Right now I'm most reluctant to discuss . . .

47

Interracial dating and/or marriage make me feel . . .

48

Premarital or extramarital sex . . .

Structured Experience 21

49

Right now this experience is making me feel . . .

50

Express how you are feeling toward your partner without using words. You may want to touch. Afterward, tell what you intended to communicate. Also, explore how this form of communication feels.

51

The thing I like best about you is . . .

52

You are . . .

53

What I think you need to know is . . .

54

Right now I'm responding to . . .

55

I want you to . . .

Time permitting, you might wish to continue this encounter through topics of your own choosing. Several possibilities are: money, religion, politics, race, marriage, the future, and the two of you.

22. NONVERBAL COMMUNICATION: A COLLECTION OF ACTIVITIES

Listed below are several nonverbal exercises that can be used in human relations laboratories. It is important to note that, like fantasy methods, these activities sometimes generate potent data. The facilitator needs to consider the points raised in the introduction to Fantasies (*Vol. I: Structured Experience 16*).

Dyadic Experiences

1. *Trust Fall.* One partner stands with his back turned to the other. With his arms extended sideways, he falls backward and is caught by his partner. They reverse roles and repeat the activity.

2. *Trust Walk.* One partner closes his eyes and is led around blind—through and over things. They reverse roles and repeat the activity.

3. *Trust Run.* Outside, one partner closes his eyes and is led by the other in a vigorous run. They reverse roles and repeat the activity.

4. *Pushing and Shoving.* Partners lock fingers, with arms extended over their heads. They push against each other, trying to drive each other to the wall.

5. *Feeling Faces.* With eyes closed, partners stand face-to-face, exploring each other's faces very gently with their hands.

6. *Progression.* Partners sit facing each other, sharing their feelings about each other verbally. After two or three minutes, they sit back-to-back and continue sharing verbally. After an additional two or three minutes they sit face-to-face again and communicate without using words.

7. *Tug-of-War.* Partners imagine a line between them on the floor and have a tug-of-war with an imaginary rope. One partner is to be pulled across the line.

8. *Patting.* Partners stand facing each other. One stands, eyes closed, with his hands at his sides. The other very gently pats both sides of his body, starting with the head and going all the way down to the feet and back up to the head. They reverse roles and repeat the activity.

9. *Mirroring.* Partners stand facing each other. One becomes the mirror image of the other's bodily movements. With hands in front, palms toward partner, they move expressively. Then one closes his eyes and attempts to mirror the slow hand movements of the other (hands almost touching.) They reverse roles and repeat the activity.

10. *Finding a Distance*. Partners locate themselves at a distance from each other and encounter each other nonverbally. They experiment until they find the most comfortable distance.

Group Experiences

11. *Roll*. Group participants stand in a tight circle. A volunteer, or a participant who wants to develop additional trust in the group, is rolled around inside the circle. He may be thrown from side to side. It is important that the person in the center keep his feet together, his knees locked, and his eyes closed.

12. *Cradle*. The group picks up a participant who is lying on his back on the floor with his eyes closed. (Support his head.) He is lifted high in the air and gently rocked back and forth. Then he is slowly lowered to the floor, and hands are removed from him very expressively.

Multi-Group Experiences

13. *Eye-Contact Chain*. Participants form two lines, facing each other about a yard apart. They hold hands, and the persons at the two ends hold hands. This forms a chain similar to a bicycle chain. Without talking, each participant establishes eye contact with the person opposite him. When the group is ready, everyone takes one step to the right. Eye contact is established with the next person. The group continues until members return to their original positions.

14. *Circles*. All participants hold hands in a large circle. They make the circle as large as possible, stretching until it almost breaks. Then they make the circle as small as possible, crowding in very close.

15. *Newspaper Hitting*. Each participant is given a rolled-up newspaper. Participants go about the room encountering each other by hitting with the newspapers.

16. *Milling*. Participants mill about the room aimlessly, eyes closed, encountering each other without using words. Variations: Open eyes (do not shake hands); or, close eyes and locate partner.

17. *Group Grope*. Participants lie on their stomachs in a circle on the floor as far from the center of the room as possible, heads toward the center. With their eyes closed, they slowly crawl into the center, forming a pile.

18. *Feeling Music*. Contrasting styles of music are played (romantic, rock, folk, etc.). Participants act out their feelings in dance.

Similar Structured Experiences: *Vol. I:* Structured Experience 7; *Vol. II:* **44, 47**; *Vol. III:* **71, 72**; *'72 Annual:* **84, 86**; *Vol. IV:* **106.**
Lecturette Source: *'72 Annual:* "Modes of Communication: An Experiential Lecture."

Notes on the use of "Nonverbal Communication":

23. COINS: SYMBOLIC FEEDBACK

Goals

I. To experiment with giving feedback symbolically.

II. To share feelings involved with giving, receiving, and rejection.

Group Size

Between eight and twelve participants.

Time Required

Approximately one-and-a-half hours.

Materials

Each participant brings a penny, a nickel, a dime, and a quarter to the group meeting.

Physical Setting

Participants are seated in a circle.

Process

I. The facilitator explains the goals of the exercise.

II. To establish an appropriate atmosphere, the facilitator leads a fantasy exercise. Participants are instructed to close their eyes and to imagine themselves as something other than persons, something they would like to be. After about two minutes, the facilitator tells his own fantasy (and why he chose to be that thing) and asks members to take turns around the circle, in a clockwise direction.

III. Participants are instructed to examine their four coins and to select one with which they can identify. (Some selection criteria are size, utility, inscriptions, denomination, composition, year, person depicted, and mint.) The other coins are put away, and each participant places the coin which he chose on the floor in front of him.

IV. Participants take turns sharing reasons for their selection of coins. The participant on the facilitator's right begins, and the process moves counterclockwise.

V. The participants then silently make an emotional commitment to give this part of themselves to another member of the group. *It is important to stress this com-*

mitment so that participants will not change it for reasons of reciprocation or compassion. Participants may *not* present their coins to the group as a whole. As soon as each participant commits himself, he places his coin on the floor in front of him.

VI. As soon as all the coins have been put on the floor, the facilitator explains the next step. Moving clockwise, participants present their coins, *i.e.*, a part of themselves, to other members. The presentation is made standing in front of the person, with eye contact.

VII. Beginning with the participant who received the most coins and working through all who received coins, each receiver shares his feelings about the experience of receiving. His comments should be directed to the giver(s).

VIII. The facilitator introduces processing of the rejection experience by making the point that rejection, however slight, is one of the most difficult emotional reactions with which we deal. Participants who did not receive coins are now asked to respond.

IX. After some time for silent reflection, the facilitator opens a discussion of the total process.

Variations

I. Instead of taking turns around the circle in steps II, IV, and VI, participants can carry out the instructions in any order they wish.

II. Participants can bring objects other than coins. These can be given as symbolic feedback.

III. More than one coin can be given by each participant. If the rejection experience is inappropriate for the goals of the group, giving more than one coin makes it more probable that each person will receive at least one.

IV. In large groups the talking in steps II and IV can be done by volunteers. The giving phase is done all at once as participants mill around the room. Processing in steps VII and VIII is done in subgroups.

Similar Structured Experiences: *Vol. I:* Structured Experience **13, 17, 18;** *Vol. II:* **42;** *Vol. III:* **57, 58;** *'72 Annual:* **86;** *'73 Annual:* **99;** *Vol. IV:* **104, 107, 114.**
Lecturette Sources: *'72 Annual:* "Communication Modes: An Experiential Lecture," "Openness, Collusion, and Feedback"; *'73 Annual:* "Johari Window."

Submitted by J. William Pfeiffer, University Associates, San Diego, California.

Structured Experience 23

Notes on the use of "Coins":

24. ASSUMPTIONS ABOUT HUMAN RELATIONS TRAINING: AN OPINIONNAIRE

Goals

I. To allow the group (in this case, a human relations training staff) to assess the degree to which it has consensus on a number of assumptions that underlie laboratory learning.

II. To assist co-facilitators in identifying each other's biases about training.

III. To discover some possible "blind spots" that the training staff may have about training.

Group Size

Unlimited.

Time Required

Minimum of one hour.

Materials

I. Copies of Opinionnaire on Assumptions About Human Relations Training for all participants.

II. Newsprint and felt-tipped marker.

III. Pencils for all participants.

Physical Setting

Participants should be seated comfortably for writing. They should be able to see the display of group results.

Process

I. Copies of the opinionnaire and pencils are distributed, and participants follow the instructions on the form.

II. When everyone has finished, the facilitator announces that tallies of responses to particular items will be made. Participants indicate which items they would like to have tallied. The facilitator makes a tally chart on newsprint with the following heading:

Item No.	5 SA	4 A	3 U	2 D	1 SD

III. Items are tallied and discussed one at a time. Particular attention is paid to items on which there is dispersion of response and to those on which there is near unanimity (possible blind spots).

IV. Co-facilitators meet to exchange their responses to items of mutual interest.

Variations

I. A shorter form of the opinionnaire can be developed by selecting items that most closely fit the goals of the training event.

II. Staff members can predict each other's responses to particular items.

III. In a personal growth laboratory, an abbreviated form of the opinionnaire can be used to elicit expectations of participants.

IV. Instead of tallying the group's responses in the session, clerks can develop staff norms during another activity, such as a meal.

V. Individuals or an ongoing training staff can use the opinionnaire several times over a long period to study changes in assumptions underlying their work.

Similar Structured Experiences: *Vol. II:* Structured Experience **48.**
Lecturette Sources: *'72 Annual:* "Guidelines for Group Member Behavior," "Risk-Taking and Error-Protection Styles," "Assumptions About the Nature of Man"; *'73 Annual:* "A Two-Phase Approach to Human Relations Training."

This structured experience was submitted by John E. Jones, University Associates, San Diego, California. The opinionnaire was prepared with the assistance of Jim Dickinson, University of South Florida, Tampa, and Carla Dee, University of Iowa, Iowa City, The normative data were derived from a 1969 survey of the membership of the Midwest Group for Human Resources conducted by John E. Jones and B. Howard Arbes, University of Wisconsin, Madison.

Notes on the use of "Assumptions About Human Relations Training":

Structured Experience 24

OPINIONNAIRE ON ASSUMPTIONS
ABOUT HUMAN RELATIONS TRAINING

Name_____   Date_____

Instructions: Assumptions about personal growth groups and participants in laboratory training are listed. Use a five-point scale: 5, strongly agree; 4, agree; 3, uncertain; 2, disagree; and 1, strongly disagree. Report your reaction to each item in the space at the left of the item number.

_____ 1. A substantial number of group participants, when confronted with others' behaviors and feelings in an atmosphere of psychological safety, can produce articulate and constructive feedback.

_____ 2. A certain degree of communality is necessary if the feedback is to be helpful for the individual.

_____ 3. The behavior emitted in the group is sufficiently representative of behavior outside the group so that learning occurring within the group will carry over or transfer.

_____ 4. Psychological safety can be achieved relatively quickly (in a matter of a few hours) either among complete strangers or among associates who have had varying types and degrees of interpersonal interaction.

_____ 5. Almost everyone initially lacks interpersonal competence; that is, individuals tend to have distorted self-images, faulty perceptions, and poor communication skills.

_____ 6. A trusting atmosphere is conducive to self-revelation.

_____ 7. People are more accepting of themselves when they perceive that others accept them.

_____ 8. Negative feedback is conducive to change.

_____ 9. People love and trust others to the extent that they love and trust themselves.

_____ 10. In understanding others better, we understand ourselves better.

_____ 11. Authenticity is desirable in personal growth groups.

_____ 12. The progress of a personal growth group is dependent upon the skill of the trainer.

_____ 13. Self-revelation is necessary for change.

_____ 14. A poor trainer/cotrainer relationship is deleterious to the functioning of a group.

_____ 15. People in the helping professions tend to underestimate the strength and resilience of normal people.

_____ 16. Most persons feel freer to change their behavior when they feel they are understood and cared for.

_____ 17. People can be seriously hurt by their experiences in a personal growth group.

_____ 18. The trainer who participates in the group to satisfy his own needs prevents the group from completing its development.

_____ 19. The conditions leading to behavior change require the person to feel frustrated or fearful.

_____ 20. Behavior changes become more or less permanent according to the person's perception of the rewards for such behavior.

_____ 21. Persons who usually are quiet in the personal growth group sessions do not get as much out of the experience as people who participate more actively.

_____ 22. People who have not cried in the personal growth group have not shared their true feelings.

_____ 23. The members of a personal growth group generally can be trusted to stop short of a participant's breaking point.

_____ 24. The value of a personal growth group experience can be justified on whatever grounds seem appropriate to any participant.

_____ 25. The personal growth group experience may decrease a person's sense of individual responsibility for what he does.

_____ 26. Personal growth group training sponsored by an institution should not produce outcomes inconsistent with the stated goals of the supporting institution.

_____ 27. Almost everyone can profit from personal growth group experience.

_____ 28. Through the personal growth group experience, you can see that all people are deserving of your love.

_____ 29. There should be no restrictions on the behavior of personal growth group participants, with the exception that no one should be allowed to strike another person with a solid object or closed fist.

_____ 30. For most people in a laboratory setting, sexual intercourse is an appropriate and desirable form of interaction.

Structured Experience 24

_____ 31. The trainer, to be effective or useful, should feel free to interact and participate just as any other participant in the group.

_____ 32. Without the introduction of theory units—either in separate sessions or, as appropriate, in personal growth group meetings—the laboratory method of teaching produces little generalizable information for the participant.

_____ 33. Nonverbal exercises are potentially useful techniques for generating additional data in a personal growth group.

_____ 34. The personal growth group's time is more productively employed by looking at and discussing the "here and now" rather than a participant's problems at home or at work.

_____ 35. People generally approach learning and change with ambivalence.

_____ 36. Immediate feedback is more useful than delayed feedback.

_____ 37. Emphasis on the "here and now" is more effective than discussion of life-history data.

_____ 38. Knowledge of one's impact on others leads to more effective interpersonal functioning.

_____ 39. Task groups which study their own process are the most effective.

_____ 40. Data-based decisions are better than intuitive (instinctive) ones.

_____ 41. Democratic decision-making results in the most effective action.

_____ 42. With regard to decision-making in groups, efficiency is less important than effectiveness.

_____ 43. As bases for decisions made in groups, feeling data are equally as important as what participants think.

_____ 44. Common problems cannot be solved well in groups without participation of those affected by the solution.

_____ 45. The final arbiter of the rightness of any collective judgment or arrangement is the procedure of consensual validation.

_____ 46. Motive analysis is to be avoided in the personal growth group.

_____ 47. One can teach another only if he can enlist the other in thinking and learning for himself.

_____ 48. Confronting a personal growth group participant with the effects of his behavior is an effective way of helping him.

_____ 49. Empathic understanding is a necessary condition for giving help.

_____ 50. The effectiveness of the trainer is more a function of his personality than it is a function of his academic preparation.

_____ 51. Competition within a group generally produces better decisions.

_____ 52. The use of taboo words is an index of the level of authenticity in the group.

_____ 53. Conflict should decrease in the human relations group as the members come to know one another better.

_____ 54. Asking for help in the human relations group appears to be more difficult for most members than giving help.

Structured Experience 24

ASSUMPTIONS ABOUT HUMAN RELATIONS TRAINING: NORMATIVE DATA

Percentage Norms°

Item No.	5 SA	4 A	3 U	2 D	1 SD	Item No.	5 SA	4 A	3 U	2 D	1 SD
1	55	38	3	3	1	28	2	10	20	47	21
2	38	21	24	11	2	29	2	7	10	51	30
3	9	43	33	12	3	30	0	0	11	43	46
4	7	37	21	29	6	31	15	33	19	26	7
5	8	36	16	30	10	32	10	30	19	34	7
6	65	31	3	1	6	33	44	52	3	1	0
7	48	43	6	1	2	34	47	46	4	2	1
8	7	44	37	10	2	35	36	50	6	6	2
9	22	49	22	6	1	36	51	41	6	2	0
10	24	52	16	6	2	37	45	46	7	1	1
11	57	39	3	6	1	38	42	47	10	1	0
12	12	45	28	14	1	39	32	49	13	5	1
13	14	31	24	26	5	40	11	39	34	15	1
14	29	44	20	6	1	41	11	36	34	16	3
15	20	49	20	10	1	42	17	45	25	11	2
16	43	50	6	1	0	43	31	57	8	3	1
17	12	42	19	23	4	44	34	53	10	2	1
18	15	28	27	26	4	45	9	29	30	23	9
19	2	21	25	37	15	46	10	30	30	28	2
20	9	54	26	9	2	47	30	50	11	8	1
21	3	28	26	33	10	48	25	64	9	1	1
22	0	2	2	34	62	49	25	46	13	13	3
23	5	49	24	16	6	50	17	40	25	15	3
24	3	22	33	27	15	51	2	20	34	36	8
25	2	18	19	42	19	52	0	5	19	52	24
26	10	13	24	34	19	53	2	18	20	48	12
27	8	35	17	33	7	54	23	58	12	6	1

°Based on results obtained from 238 experienced group facilitators—71% of those contacted.

SOURCES OF ADDITIONAL STRUCTURED EXPERIENCES

Gunther, B. *Sense Relaxation: Below Your Mind.* New York: Collier Books, 1968.

Gunther, B. *What to Do Till the Messiah Comes.* New York: Collier Books, 1971.

James, M., and D. Jongeward. *Born to Win: Transactional Analysis with Gestalt Experiments.* Reading, Mass.: Addison-Wesley, 1971.

Jones, J.E., and J.W. Pfeiffer. *The 1973 Annual Handbook for Group Facilitators.* University Associates, 1973.

Lewis, H., and H. Streitfield. *Growth Games.* New York: Bantam, 1971.

Maier, N.R.F., A.R. Solem, and A.A. Maier. *Supervisory and Executive Development: A Manual for Role Playing.* New York: Wiley, 1967.

Malamud, D.I., and S. Machover. *Toward Self-Understanding: Group Techniques in Self-Confrontation.* Springfield, Ill.: Thomas, 1965.

NTL Institute for Applied Behavioral Science. *Twenty Exercises for Trainers.* Washington, D.C., 1972.

Nylen, D., J.R. Mitchell, and A. Stout (editors). *Handbook of Staff Development and Human Relations Training: Materials Developed for Use in Africa* (revised edition). Washington, D.C.: NTL Institute for Applied Behavioral Science, 1967.

Otto, H.A. *Group Methods to Actualize Human Potential: A Handbook* (second edition). Beverly Hills: Holistic Press, 1970.

Pfeiffer, J.W., and R. Heslin. *Instrumentation in Human Relations Training: A Guide to 75 Instruments with Wide Application to the Behavioral Sciences.* University Associates, 1973.

Pfeiffer, J.W., and J.E. Jones. *A Handbook of Structured Experiences for Human Relations Training, Volumes II* (revised), *III* (revised), and *IV.* University Associates, 1974, 1974, and 1973.

Pfeiffer, J.W., and J.E. Jones. *The 1972 Annual Handbook for Group Facilitators.* University Associates, 1972.

atir, V. *Conjoint Family Therapy: A Guide to Theory and Technique.* Palo Alto, Ca.: Science and Behavior Books, 1967.

Schmuck, R.A., P.J. Runkel, *et al. Handbook of Organization Development in Schools.* Palo Alto, Ca.: National Press Books, 1972.

Schutz, W.C. *Joy: Expanding Human Awareness.* New York: Grove Press, 1967.